# ERGONOMIC
# Mis-ADVENTURES

Ian Chong CPE

*Certified Professional Ergonomist*

*Dedicated to:*
*Bruce Wong PE, Jim Bowen JD,*
*Gene Alban MD, Dieter Jahns CPE*
*Gen. John Stanford*
*Real Mentors & Friends, Whom I Miss Terribly*
*They Taught Me How to Laugh & Learn*

Special thanks to Karl Marion CIE CPE, Gary Orr CPE
Alan Hedge PhD CPE, for help, friendship & support

# What Others Are Saying About the Author and This Book

*Plenty of great examples for job improvement. A valuable resource for workers, novice ergonomist and the ergo pro. Enlightening and informative, a joy to read. The case studies and applications show how valuable ergonomics really is.*

**Gary Orr, PE, CPE - Ergonomist**
**US Department of Labor**

*Great insight to practical applications for prevention and solving of worker injury. An important book showing the difference between Voodoo and Real Ergonomics. I had no idea Ergonomics could go this deep and be this important and beneficial.*

**Sabrina Sanchez – President**
**The Ventana Group**

*A must read for all those practicing in the ergonomics field. Ian's take on 'voodoo ergonomics' is hard hitting and will open your eyes. It makes you think deeper about the science and laugh at the same time.*

**Lance Perry PE CPE - Senior Ergonomist**
**Risk Engineering / AHP Ergonomics**
**Zurich Services Corporation**

*A lively, entertaining, thoughtful and provocative book on the importance of Ergonomics. Enlightening and informative, a great read. A valuable resource for anyone who wants to prevent workplace injuries and boosts productivity. Richly illustrated with case studies and applications to show how valuable ergonomics really is to any business.*

**Prof. Alan Hedge MS, PhD, CPE, FHFES, FIEFH, FIEA**
**Director, Human Factors & Ergonomics Lab**
**Cornell University**

*Mr. Chong really understands the application of ergonomics in all realms of occupational injury. Of special note is the appreciation of design elements in ergonomic applications and their benefits. A truly revealing book.*

**Jon Biggs – Dir. Sales & Marketing**
**Kinesis Corporation**

# What Others Are Saying About the Author and This Book

*Chong obviously approaches his work with passion and commitment. His work can only describe him as "incredible, in terms of the human aspect of his work in helping people overcoming industrial injuries.*
### Judy Margles – Former Curator
### Oregon Museum of Science and Industry

*This valuable reference takes ergonomics from an often misunderstood science to an applied, practical and fun level. A necessary reference for ergonomic teams and leaders who desire the true meaning and application of ergonomics.*
### Wayne Maynard CSP CPE - Product Director-Worker Compensation Ergonomics & Tribology
### Liberty Mutual Insurance

*Ergonomic Mis-Adventures best describes the author's style in presenting a subject not easily translated to the reading public. Prepare to enjoy an insightful, entertaining immersion into the science of ergonomics." Great read!*
### Brian Ducey – Director
### SMART Association

*Ian is undoubtedly one of the most creative ergonomists I have ever had the pleasure to interact with!*
### Sue Rodgers
### Consultant in Ergonomics

*Entertaining and sometimes disquieting, a good and provocative read. It's an impassioned plea for Ergo Pros to have a personal commitment to doing ergonomics. Well thought-out especially the head-shaking examples of "ergonomics and ergonomic products. A funny yet educational and occasionally uncomfortable review of the lessons Chong has learned in his vast experience. It challenges the standard or perceived role of ergonomics.*
### Steve Morrissey PhD CPE - Senior Ergonomist
### Oregon OSHA

*Hilarious and creative writings about a serious subject, bringing to light relatively unknown but important concepts. Truly enlightening for anyone involved in the science. HIGHLY RECOMMENDED!*
### Julie Landis - President
### Ergo Concepts LLC

Cover design by Brian Jack Farris
Stock Graphics & Clipart courtesy of:
        Clker.com, Dreamstime.com & Graphicstock.com
        (unless otherwise noted)
Sketches / drawings mostly by the Author +


Printed by CreateSpace, An Amazon.com Company

ISBN - 13: 978-1508663034
ISBN - 10:1508663033

# About the Author

**_Ian Chong is a real life,_** award winning, vastly experienced (*lots of gray hairs*), highly credentialed (*plenty of boot marks on the back side*), Certified Professional Ergonomist *AND* performing Magician, with an outstanding sense of humor, albeit somewhat nerdy.

Educated in Ergonomics & Occupational Biomechanics (NYU); Industrial Design (Pratt Institute, NYC); Architecture (UWash), and Inventing (School of Hard Knocks); he is known for RUGGED, MACHO, GRIMY industrial Ergonomics and complex office Ergonomics. You can find him (often in his shop – preferable to his office) developing creative solutions, getting workers out of pain and helping companies add to their bottom line.

A self proclaimed **_"tool junkie"_** he feels returning anyone back to work despite any injury or preventing any injury proactively is really quite easy.

You only need a solid approach, a little design creativity and you too can develop solutions for any complex / difficult occupations, including musicians, industry workers, police officers, construction workers, heavy machine operators, cooks, plus thousands of others. Need some inspiration? Give him a poke -**WWW.ERGOINC.COM.**

He also heartwarmingly admits to receiving many Starbuck lattes and gifts from the company store in thanks from workers, helping them keep their jobs, supporting families.

Other than the coloring books filled in when a kid, Ergonomic Mis-Adventures is his second real book.

# Disclaimer

*I am FIRMLY of the opinion that NO product is universally "Ergonomic", and that it is best to have a TRAINED, EXPERIENCED OR CREDENTIALED Ergonomist to select the best products for specific situations and application!*

*Otherwise you are simply shooting in the dark and probably won't even come close to hitting the target.*

There are those who would think simply because I have included specific products in this book that I am endorsing them and may even be on the manufacturers' payroll for such. Let it be known that these mentions are **_NOT_** a product promotion in any way!

Let me say here emphatically and unequivocally that even though several specific products appear in this book, that I am only illustrating our projects and showing some successes, yes and even critique of them. The point is to demonstrate how these products can be used to the advantage of businesses and mostly for the reduction of someone's pain.

Even though not endorsing them in any way, I am pleased to demonstrate the positive results we have had with them and state the reasons why. And yes, some of them work wonderfully well, (and this is key) in the right application.

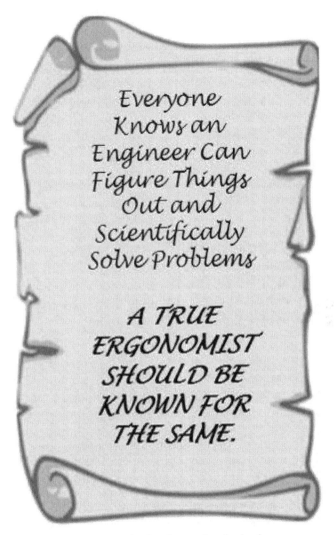

Everyone Knows an Engineer Can Figure Things Out and Scientifically Solve Problems

A TRUE ERGONOMIST SHOULD BE KNOWN FOR THE SAME.

Are you a worker in pain or on the other hand,
are you one of the professionals who can help these folks get out of pain?

# Introduction - con't

**Ergonomics affects you, personally**, right here, right now, whether you know it or not.  It can affect you well or badly in important ways.  Hands, wrists, shoulders, neck or back on fire?  Probably from bad Ergonomics resulting in bad workstations or work tasks, no matter what it is that you do.  It contributes to happy or gloomy outlooks, or endless wells of frustration.  <u>*But, Ergonomics can also really help you or someone else.*</u> It's entirely up to you!

*It is currently a vastly misunderstood, misquoted, misaligned, and a highly undervalued field of knowledge.*

What do you honestly know about Ergonomics?  Most folks know the word, but not much else.  **Let this be a guide book, designed for the Worker in Pain and Ergo Pro of any level for clearing up questions, myths and confusion about Ergonomics**.  This is <u>**NOT**</u> a textbook.  No fancy charts, no big words, no scientific jargon.  This is a real world, applications and how-to book.  It's about real people having real problems in real pain, how to get out of it, and a call out of those who make those problems and pain worse.

It will show you how Ergonomics is a serious subject that can fully impact someone's career, life and ultimately their entire future in a big positive way!

Inside are clues, stories, roadmaps, mishaps and philosophies on how to solve tough complex Ergo problems for perilous at-risk computer and heavy duty industrial work stations.  This represents a mini Ergo course, sharing professional trade secrets uncovered from a long career in the trenches and maybe even inspiring an Ergo career in some way. But most of all there is, I hope, a sense of wonder, amazement and humor about the wonderful science of Ergonomics and how it can help people.

Inside you will find things that will:

- Provide simple real life advice on how to take care of yourself and your pain at work
- Show you where Ergonomics can take us and why it's important to people and the business world
- Help & inspire those involved in the Ergo world
- Uncover hidden secrets in Ergonomics applications

*But mostly these writings here are a call out to those in the profession to look inside themselves and make effort to UP THEIR GAME for the benefit of all.*

Unfortunately there is also a ***"dark" or sad side, almost a dangerous side*** that should be revealed to those unaware.

## *The Bad Stuff or DARK Side*

This book exists because this wonderful craft is in danger of being turned into something laughable. This "DARK" side is doing vast amounts of harm from those jumping on the opportunity bandwagon without proper training, proper credentialing or oftentimes a lack of conscience.

# Introduction - con't

Known as Kindergarten or Voodoo Ergonomists, they circulate among workplaces doing cut rate work. In fact, often workers roll their eyes or flinch when the word Ergonomics is spoken, probably because of a bad experience with one of these so-called Ergonomists.

These cut-raters often try, but don't take it far enough. Even having the potential, skill and intellect to help workers in pain they simply failed. They just don't do enough and essentially abandon those who they were chartered to help. That person they were to help was short changed, shortening their career, compromising their quality of life and ultimately their future and to top it off, just left to simply deal with their pain on their own (See Chapter III – Snake Oil Ergonomics).

\*\*\*

Ergonomics got a lot of publicity and a really bad rap a few years back when OSHA (Occupational Safety and Health Administration) attempted to create a well-meaning set of Ergonomics standards. Those regulations attempted to make a science of human variability into a set of black and white rules. Other legislative mishaps took Ergonomics out of science and into politics. Media hype then put Ergonomics into a laughable limelight by spreading fear into business owners and workers on the job.

Adding to the confusion, advertisers began using the term as a catch phrase describing their products. It became a technical buzzword, twisted, bent and falsified into pure advertising deceptions attempting to give products more pizzazz, more flash.

## *The Good Stuff*

Good, serious, real Ergonomics are presented here and their beneficial impact on workers in pain and businesses. Knowledge and proper application of the science is empowering. Many tools are included, just for the asking.

## So let this book be a call.

By shedding light on the harm bad Ergonomics does, both the disrespect and potentially vast benefits of Ergonomics are seen. In this way I hope to inspire those of you true to the art to take up the flag and *place Ergonomics where it should be in the high echelons of healthcare and also as a pure business tool.*

I implore anyone who has an interest to further your skillsets - take up this noble profession and help people, but you can't do it haphazardly. You need proper training, experience and analytical skills. Like any other profession you have to do it right, really right. Most people don't.

## So I'm asking…Really Asking

Want a mentor? Give me a call, anytime. Open invitation. Email is in the back.

# A Special Note to Readers

*I don't care if you are a doctor, janitor, accountant, secretary, home-maker, carpenter, or whatever, if you purposefully and effectively take away someone's pain, not simply addressing symptomology, while they are doing something important to them (occupational or recreational), then you are indeed performing Ergonomics at the highest level.*

## And for this you have my everlasting admiration!

In advancing Ergonomics to out-of-the-box thinking, our firm became known for doing:

*Macho, Rugged often Grimy Creative Ergonomics.*

We have improved many lives and helped secure the future and careers of many injured workers, and for that we are very proud.

Although there is some calling out of snake oilers and voodooists in the following pages, *I strongly feel:*

*You do not necessarily need to be a highly credentialed Ergonomist to take away someone's pain. If you simply do that, you too can have the same high level impact on a lot of lives, helping secure the future and careers of many injured workers…and for that, you too can be very proud.*

# Table of Contents

# Fantasy, Fun
# &
# Soapbox Stories

Someday Ergonomics will be so well understood, appreciated and in the forefront in everyone's mind that it will deserve a place in mainstream advertising.

Here is an Ergo Fantasy as it would appear on Prime Time TV.

# Ergonomics Fantasy
## (Someday to be "As seen on TV")

### Hi, I'm (your name),
### The worlds greatest Ergonomist

Now pulling 150# manhole covers or shoveling wet snow like Jeff and Bill here are back breaking jobs.

And for back breaking jobs you need Serious Ergonomics So Jeff & Bill have the right tools to perform these tasks without seriously injuring themselves.

*They can save their health, work longer, improve productivity And most importantly support their families.*

### But for those every day minor aches and pains,
### You need Tylenol / Bufferin / Aleve etc.

### Now back to the important work of helping folks with their injuries.

## Chapter I

# Hollywood Ergonomics & Mainstream Media

New York Time Bestseller featuring
Ergonomic equipment
(Author's Collection)

007 Action bringing Ergonomics to the
Silver Screen
(Author's DVD Collection)

Road & Track Magazine featuring
Bugatti Veyron 16.4 - Jan 2006
(Author's Collection)

Futuristic Ergonomics
(Author's DVD Collection)

## Yes, Ergonomics is Finally Introduced in Mass Media & Pop Culture
*(Starring in all of these and more)*

*Public acceptance and understanding about relatively unknown subjects including **Ergonomics** is almost nonexistent, remaining in the shadows, misunderstood, misapplied, and often associated with less than stellar meanings.*

However, you know when a term or item is on the way to hitting the mainstream American lexicon when it appears in pop culture, magazines, newspapers and in a highly visible Hollywood movie or best seller adventure book. Ergonomics has been slowly creeping into mainstream media for the past several years.

Witness the stylized Kinesis Contoured™ keyboard; with some futuristic science fiction type movies have placed it in a starring role.

(Authors DVD Collection

Take the Men in Black movie series. In the super secret surveillance control room with scads of high tech futuristic machinery, what is the futuristic keyboard of choice? None other than the Kinesis Contoured™ keyboard. It looks sexy and futuristic, and if you have never seen one before, it definitely looks like something out of a science fiction toy catalog. And in close examination, by virtue of its design and function it is, of course, Ergonomic.

In this scene taken from the movie, MIB Agent K (Tommy Lee Jones) is in the MIB control room with the Kinesis Contoured™ keyboard
Note – hand and forearm positioning

In one scene Agent K (Tommy Lee Jones) can be seen inputting data with the Kinesis keyboard, although he's got poor placement of the monitor (to the side) and keyboard (too high). In wide screen shots of the control room and various agents at their high tech desks, the Kinesis Contoured$^{TM}$ can be definitely if not fleetingly recognized being used to track the various aliens and happenings that Tommy and Will Smith protect us from. In the screen shot above, Mr. Jones clearly rests his palms, not wrists on the oversized palm rests eliminating any pressure on his carpal tunnel which will undoubtedly help in his tasks tracking and fighting the aliens.

Alas, on to another fantasy film: Disney's .,

# FLUBBER

Not the Old 1961 Flubber (Absent Minded Professor) with Fred MacMurray flying in his Flubber powered Model A...

But in the New Green Flubber with the late Robin Williams

Flubber starring the late Robin Williams portraying the eccentric professor / inventor Prof. Philip Brainard is a fantasy (it's Disney) movie with fun high tech action. The Kinesis Contoured$^{TM}$ shows up at the good Professor's computer workstation. Trusty sidekick floating robot Weebo (Jody Benson) is shown to input into the computer, making a fantasy companion for the Professor, (although not touching the keyboard, she simply uses bluray).

In the movie, the Professor's hands can be seen performing rapid input to resurrect the damaged Weebo. The keyboard is doing what I think is significant in addressing some of the hand / wrist / forearm issues seen in power keyboarders. In Ergonomic terms, the "split" keeps the hands apart, eliminating the inward arm rotation required to type on a straight keyboard orientation, and the indented space for the key allow a posture with the knuckles below the forearm.

Also, the big palm rests effectively remove problematic pressure on the underside of the wrists. Using a typical wrist rest or using the edge of the desk does indeed place pressure on the underside of the wrists exactly where the carpal tunnel is, so don't let anyone tell you that wrist rests are good for you. After all the medical definition of carpal tunnel syndrome (CTS) is damage caused by the constriction of or pressure against the median nerve as it passes through the carpal tunnel.

This pressure also puts tendons and tendon sheaths in duress while they pass through or near by the carpal tunnel. The Kinesis Contoured™ with its oversized palm rests puts pressure on the big fleshy parts of the palm (thenar and hypothenar eminences) with less peril to wrist structures. Thus helping reduce the risk of carpal tunnel syndrome, facilitating healing of tendonitis and tenosynovitis conditions. All the while reducing pain and allowing power keyboarders to more easily function through breakneck keyboarding tasks.

This particular keyboard does things typical keyboards can only hope for. Not only does it look cool, but it functions well to boot. The remapped keyboard moves the high usage <enter>, <backspace>, <tab> and <esc> keys from at-risk outward turning of both hands (ulnar deviation) using the small fingers to a central location for thumb usage. This repositioning can offload a significant cause of hand / wrist problems.

Naturally its sexy good looks, shape and form not only got it into a blockbuster movie, but its well-thought-out functions got it into a prominent place in the Ergonomics world. It's a great keyboard to have in your toolbox when addressing complex hand, wrist and arm maladies / biomechanical challenges. *All in all, a nice piece of design with well thought out Ergonomics, but remember, it's not for everyone. Like the late Vince Lombardi once said:* **"Application is not everything, it's the ONLY thing,"** *(modified for the circumstances, of course).*

# Tom Clancy's NetForce Ergonomics

Starring Scott Bakula as Alex Michaels and
Joanna Going as Toni Fiorelli -circa 1999

Another Kinesis keyboard had a cameo role in the
Tom Clancy TV movie NetForce. The overall
Ergonomic humor in this movie is that the good
guys use the Kinesis keyboards, and the bad guys
use a keyboard without Ergo features.

The main gist of the movie is the chasing down of
an Internet baddie who wants to hack into any
computer controlling the Word Wide Web. Steve
Day (actor Kris Kristofferson) plays the head of the
new FBI Counter Internet Terrorism Group called
NetForce with Alex Michaels (Scott Bakula)
playing his 1$^{st}$ lieutenant, chasing down the bad
guys.

Typical espionage bad guy vs. good guy TV action,
using two different models of Kinesis keyboards.
The first instance, the white Kinesis Contoured$^{TM}$ is
seen with Alex Michaels (Bakula), along with his
sidekick Toni Fiorelli (Joanna Going) in the
operation's car back seat, which in itself is kind of
an odd place for a full size keyboard.

However, further along in the movie, Alex (love that
name) is corresponding with his boss Steve Day
(Kristofferson) via SKYPE on a big screen. There
is a great low frontal shot (shown) of Bakula using
the now unavailable Kinesis Evolution$^{TM}$ (retired to
keyboard heaven in 2005). The keyboard is
physically split into two sections and the view is
like looking up at a king who has his hands
separated and resting on the throne arm rests. The
Evolution$^{TM}$ had two integrated touch pad pointing
devices integrated into the keyboard's inner edges
eliminating the need to widen the chair arm
platforms for a mouse or trackball, illustrated in the
photos below. It also eliminated the need for

outward rotation of the arm to use a mouse, or trackball located off to the side (see photos).

This is the way a king sits at his throne with hands majestically placed palms down on the ends of the throne armrests

This scene taken from the movie had Alex (Bakula) in a majestic pose, using the retired Kinesis Evolution split keyboard allowing a "kingly" posture with lots of keyboard control

Kinesis Evolution™ application for worker having inward arm rotation difficulties & unable to use a regular keyboard

Evolution™ allows full upright position (kingly posture) with full contact to chair back & vertical upper arm - impressive posture

It works well, especially with those having inward arm rotation problems either from shoulder impingements, or too large a body mass and girth.

In the actual case photos shown jus under Mr. Bakula, the Evolution$^{TM}$ was used because the worker had a genetic abnormality in her rib cage limiting arm inward rotation. She simply could not use a standard keyboard. Custom platforms were built for this lass and she's still using them to this day continuing to work at a job "she loves", which was in peril with her previous workstation set-up, (in which case keyboarding with inward arm rotation was intolerable).

Unfortunately, not even Scott Bakula could save the life of the Evolution$^{TM}$, but we might find him using one in his New Orleans CSI series.

Suffice it to say Kinesis is or at least should be in every good Ergonomists tool kit and at least trialed by anyone who has hand / wrist / forearm pain from lengthy bouts of keyboarding.

Who knows what inventions will come next. Perhaps if some of you creative types invent a fantastic *Ergonomic* doo-dad, you too can become a movie star or celebrity by association.

# Ergonomics in Entertainment Literature

The term *Ergonomic* is also beginning to show up in Clive Cussler adventure novels starring hero Juan Cabrillo and teammates aboard the super secret spy freighter *the Oregon*. The Oregon is described being a cleverly disguised tramp steamer to fool the bad guys. Underneath the derelict looking hull and various ship functions, is a high tech futuristically armed ship that can move at mach speed through the water and out gun any missile cruiser in any of the world navies. The Crew quarters and conference room and other areas of the Oregon are described as overly plush with original art on the walls, sparing no cost in interior design.

Obviously unlimited budgets allow the best chairs known to man. In scenes where Cabrillo is calling a conference with his teammates (he's the chairman), he is described sitting in his *Ergonomic* chair. Now, one book (Mirage) doesn't describe whether any of the other characters, gunners, executive officers or scientists, get Ergonomic chairs, or even if there are indeed other Ergonomic chairs distributed around the conference table, but the one passage in Mirage does make it a point that Chairman Cabrillo "sits in his *Ergonomic*" chair. I guess rank has its privileges.

Now adding to the plot, sitting in an Ergonomic chair obviously allows one to concentrate better with improved productivity, even enhancing performance. To this end, it is obvious that Cabrillo and his team have all the elements to dispense with any nagging discomfort and not even think or bother with any type of physical pain. Man, these chairs may even take away some severe aches and pains developed by field agents from their breakneck adventures in jungle, desert, underwater or whatever warfare that undoubtedly takes its toll on the physique...just like industrial athletes seen all the time.

The Ergonomic chairs aboard the Oregon undoubtedly take away so much pain from their butts and backs that the conferences Cabrillo and his team have elicit clear thinking. This occurs without being sidetracked by any occupational injury (see above) that whatever plan or plot they are devising is clearly thought out and will undoubtedly trash the bad guys and save the world. Cabrillo is a hero and not just because he knows how to use Ergonomics to empower creative and tactical thinking.

**Here are the passages:**

In this particular storyline, obviously more budget is allocated for interior design with the board room described having a dozen comfortable Ergonomic chairs. Yes unlimited funding from covert CIA bankrolls is quite impressive.

From Clive Cussler's Oregon Adventure "The Jungle", page 234 (hardcover).

*"Juan was the first to arrive in the boardroom. The thick glass table could seat a dozen comfortably on black leather Ergonomic chairs"*

A New York Times best seller
introducing *Ergonomics*
into thriller genre readings
(Author's hardcover collection)

From Clive Cussler's Oregon Adventure "Mirage", page 117 (hardcover):

*"Cabrillo leaned back in his Ergonomic chair, lacing his fingers behind his stubbed head."*

Clearly high stature writers like Clive Cussler undoubtedly sit in Ergonomic chairs authoring books, becoming very aware of Ergonomic benefits. This shows that at the very least the term Ergonomics is on its way to becoming more widely accepted and thankfully better understood. There are also those who may inadvertently provide some tongue-in-cheek viewpoints of such things as Ergonomic chairs. Fast forward to the end of the chapter if this intrigues you.

Another New York Times best seller introducing
*Ergonomics* into thriller genre readings
(Author's hardcover collection)

Author Clive Cussler allows Chairman Juan Cabrillo the opportunity to use Ergonomic chairs to elicit productive, clear and creative thinking in the conference room meetings.

It seems the author; Mr. Cussler obviously has experience with good and bad chairs and writes about them here, obviously understanding and experiencing the benefits of using one himself. The Oregon is apparently stocked with the best weaponry, personnel, food, equipment and even the best *Ergonomic* chairs in the conference room. Who knows, perhaps Mr. Cussler will eventually include some fantastical weaponry or futuristic equipment with futuristic *Ergonomics* described. Kudos to Mr. Cussler, he writes like an imagineer / writer I'd love to have lunch with. Mr. Cussler, are you listening?

Interestingly enough Mr. Cussler's other hero Dirk Pitt maintained a large collection of antique and racy automobiles. However, there was never a mention about the application of *Ergonomics*, even though Road & Track and Car & Driver magazines (that no doubt Dirk Pitt reads) have begun to write about the application or non-application to high end and high priced racy sports cars, even pointing out the absence of *Ergonomic* design (see section of Exotic car Ergo later in this chapter).

Perhaps we will see Mr. Cussler find some or lack of unique undiscovered applied Ergonomics in one of Dirk Pitt's vintage autos. Being a sometime gear head, I would look forward to reading that or even better, would love to help out with that!

# James Bond *Ergonomics*

007 Action bringing Ergonomics to the Silver Screen
(Author's DVD Collection)

In the James Bond Movie - Die Another Day (circa
2002). The term *Ergonomic* pops up at the most
opportune time. Unfortunately, studly James Bond
(actor Pierce Brosnan) is not the one who utters the
magic word. Nor is it the lovely Jinx (actress Halle
Berry). Their nemesis Gustav Graves (actor Toby
Stephens) does. Not quite as cool having Bond or
Berry saying it but at least the word / concept has
again hit the big screen albeit fleetingly, but
thankfully in the right context. There weren't too
many folks in the audience laughing when the word
was spoken. Mainly it was just me and my family.

The scene develops like this:

Flying high above the earth in a really fancy cargo plane, the bad guy, Gustav Graves (who used gene therapy to change his appearance from one of Asian ancestry to the appearance of Occidental ancestry) is about to unleash a solar powered death ray onto the world for his own gain. His faithful companion (actually a gofer / assistant / personal long haired scruffy scientist); Vladimir Popov (actor Michael Gorevoy), brings an aluminum suitcase to the control room and sets it on a table for the bad guy, (Graves) to use. The suitcase naturally contains a high tech control system to be used for setting off a big death ray.

This is probably what it looked like:

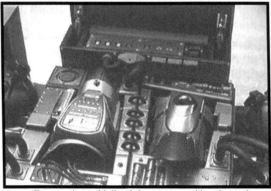

A non Ergonomic world dissolving ray control box in a suitcase
Just like a fancy X-Box console

You would think that any control designer worth his salt would even at the very basic level give some thought to the *Ergonomics* of such a critical piece of control equipment. However, in real life, the control panel of nuclear power plants (Three Mile Island) shows that this sometimes just doesn't happen.

Remember the movie China Syndrome with Jane Fonda, Michael Douglas and Jack Lemmon? A great movie, China Syndrome was coincidentally released 12 days before the Three Mile Island Nuclear Catastrophe in 1979 and won numerous awards, perhaps because of the actual fear factor and real life occurrences.

China Syndrome starring
"Three Mile Island" with Michael Douglas,
Jane Fonda & Jack Lemmon
©MARTINLISNER / Dreamstime.com

Author's DVD Collection

Studies of complex control panels show that the operators themselves color code and map out critical links on switches, dials and readouts with colored tape and magnets (see following photos).

# The *Scary* Real World Lack of Ergonomics

Below is an example of operators mapping out relationships of controls with colored tape and magnetic strips. Without these additions I don't know if anyone could keep track of what's what in a nuclear power plant, let alone how to identify a dangerous condition and where or what it actually is. Chernobyl and Three Mile Island operator interviews revealed healthy dread of not being in control from sensory overload in emergency situations when the entire control panel lights up like Broadway. Pure and abject fear seems to be a commonality. Not surprising.

An overloaded complex system of indicators and switches on which the operators themselves mapped out their relationships to each other simply to minimize confusion, especially in emergency situations

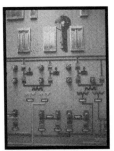

Here's what some operators did to make sense of the complex indicators and switches at Three Mile Island Nuclear Power Plant

[4] Control panel of the B&W Lynchburg simulator, sim
but not identical to that at TMI, shows the pressure, an
pressurizer level recorders and steam table. No steam
was used at TMI. Recorders are identified in the fold-o
opposite p. 42. The instrument glare shown occurs at
normal illumination.

Article showing problem at Three Mile Island
control panels, abysmal results from lack of
Ergonomics

Creative applications showing how operators
practice their own brand of Ergonomics by
installing Heineken & Michelob switch
handles

***Enough of scary real world Lack of Ergonomics - Back to our Bond….James Bond movie:***

Upon opening the suitcase and making ready to blow up part of Korea, Graves peruses the array of controls. He makes a face reflecting angst, frustration, and disgust, realizing his gofer, the inept Vladimir Popov has once again failed him or at least hasn't performed up to Graves's standards.

C'mon Dude! Doncha know what real Ergonomics is? So do some will ya?

The next cartoon character shows what Gustave Graves face looked like when he immediately blurts out in a somewhat condescending way:

*"Vlad, doesn't the word Ergonomics mean anything to you?*

*"Man machine interface?"*

*"This is still a suitcase… Finish it will you?"*

At which time Vlad looks like this. Being
confused, hurt and beaten up he remains closed
mouthed and seems like he's going to melt into
the floor...Poor Vlad, Don't you feel sorry for
him? NOT! You'll have to review the movie to
get the full impact.

If you really analyze and translate what Gustav
Graves is ranting about, it might read something
like this:

> *"Man, you sure did a crappy job of*
> *designing this to fit my genetically*
> *altered manly hands, and how am I*
> *going to take over the world if this*
> *here control system is so inadequately*
> *designed, HUH?" So get off your*
> *duff and make it Ergonomically*
> *better. COMPRENDEZ?*

Well, if applied to reality, how could anyone possibly blow up the world if the control gadget were not designed with *Ergonomic* or Human Factors principles in mind? Clearly one could not correctly select the proper parameters if the indicating lights were not the right colors or in the right sequence. Nor could one even hold the joy stick properly and move bomb sights or whatever to the right kill zone if it were not fitted specifically to his palmar warts or wrinkles. Conversely, if the labeling were not large enough or even in the right language (Korean or English in this case) how could anyone possibly push the right activation switch?

Clearly bad *Ergonomics* were to blame and poor Vlad did not have the appropriate background, either in design or *Ergonomics* to put together such a precise terrorist device and was called to the carpet in front of millions. He had absolutely no comeback or excuse for Graves' cutting remark. What a shame. But I guess he deserved it for being so ***Ergonomically Incompetent***.

For those interested in Ergo things and high level Bond adventures, this movie is great and a must see.

# Behind the Silver Screen Ergonomics

Now that you've seen Ergonomics on the big Silver Screen (even though a fantasy world), I'll bet you are wondering if Ergonomics had anything to do with actually getting it there.

Here Real World Ergonomics is shown having a lot to do with your enjoying your popcorn entertainment.

During my research, I ran into Steve Kaplan, a highly acclaimed Primetime EMMY Award winning scoring engineer. Quite an accomplishment. His work shows up in TV and Movies including DaVinci's Demons, Muppets, Agents of Shield, Crazy Stupid Love, and Black Sails. You get the picture (pun intended).

Glued to a complex audio workstation, he manipulates things acoustic / music to heighten your movie awareness manipulating your senses allowing you to actually "feel' or experience the visuals. Ever watched a movie without the sound score? If you have, you really understand how important his work is.

Naturally he works 90 hour weeks in full concentration at his workstation pictured following. He also has a young family, further squeezing his precious social and professional time.

Needless to say, like many of us, he tries to compress as much as possible out of every single hour. Short cuts here, short cuts there, all in the interest to meet crippling deadlines and of course to gain more time with his new family.

Here, we are addressing pure productivity in the realm of a high powered professional world. Personal world Ergonomics is an entirely different matter. Throw in the fact that in Mr. Kaplan's world, everything has to be perfect.

Saving precious man-seconds is critical to his occupation, in deadlines, project completion and time for final reviews. Time saved also translates into time available for his new family.

No mistakes here, perfection is not the key, *it is highly expected.* You don't get that good by being fast and sloppy using bad tools. Like any other craftsman, he needs to make every second count and make it count significantly. Add breakneck deadlines, staring at big monitors and manipulating cursors, the specter of the insidious repetitive motion industrial injury is obviously ever present, ready to strike.

The last thing a high powered computer, instrumentation user like Steve needs is a painful debilitating carpal tunnel syndrome or tendinitis slowing him down or forcing mistakes. I don't think voice activation is yet at a level to do what he needs to do for a career.

Here's Steve Kaplan's really high powered audio workstation with Kensington Trackball

ACADEMY OF TELEVISION
ARTS & SCIENCES

2012 - 2013 PRIMETIME EMMY AWARDS

HONORS

STEVE KAPLAN
Scoring Engineer

FOR CONTRIBUTIONS TO THE EMMY AWARD
WINNING ACHIEVEMENT

OUTSTANDING ORIGINAL MAIN TITLE THEME MUSIC

DA VINCI'S DEMONS

Steve Kaplan's EMMY award acknowledgement for DaVinci's Demons 2012-2013

When he started his profession, he was using a standard mouse and began developing some tell tale wrist pain. Knowing he needed to do something proactively to prevent any crippling pain or injury, he went on a mission. He abandoned the typical computer mouse and tried every conceivable input device known to man. Some were major players in the industry, being highly advertised units. Some were flash in the pan devices and like many "Ergonomic" things promising big and delivering less than nothing. Steve really understanding snake oil, settled on one of my favorites The Kensington Trackball. A favorite simply because we have found it addresses the issue of occupational injury quiet well, if it applies directly to what you are doing concerning cursor or graphics control.

At work Steve needs to be on his monitor moving, shifting and manipulating things by cursor control all the time. He's on the trackball sometimes 10 hours of the day.

Early on, Steve found one overriding factor similar to others I have seen in my career. This is experiencing any type of distraction or irritation (physical in this sense) really has a detrimental effect on the psyche (creativity in this sense). Steve found that any type of pain, even moderate pain that he "thought wouldn't bother him", would have minimal effect on his thought process. Well, he thought wrong and found different. He found that any type of hand / wrist pain greatly affected his creative process and negatively affected his work.

Even with the minor pain, he was distracted from his real "work" being creative manipulation of music within a film. His work requires high concentration on often very subtle sounds and fine audio nuances. He cannot do this if some part of his anatomy, namely his wrists are screaming "I need attention." He took it upon himself to shut down these screaming demons affecting his work.

Ever tried to go to work with a toothache? You didn't get much done I'll wager. The only thing you probably thought of was how to get to the nearest dentist. That is what happens to a creative person like Steve. He knew he had to put a stop to his wrists crying for attention and get his creative moxie back on track.

Steve likes the trackball simply because he doesn't have to locate and grip a mouse. Less action, wear and tear, or force on the palmar wrists. He doesn't like to push the typical mouse buttons with index or ring fingers, he knows it's bad. In short he uses the track ball as hand therapy. Most of all, freedom from static loading, static motion and other wrist damaging postures helps him to make your movie, TV or gaming experience more pleasurable.

Steve did something about his pain and took steps to ensure his own and valued lieutenants important careers involving high usage of cursor manipulation were not cut short by debilitating occupational injury. He standardized his entire studio with the trackballs, and I admire him for having the foresight and fortitude to do this.

You should thank him the next time you eat popcorn at the local cinema. You should appreciate the score and appreciate his efforts and be thankful he can perform them without wrist pain.

**I certainly do!**

# Television & Laugh Track Ergonomics

Now residing in TV land heaven, the cancelled TV sit com *Happy Endings*, exhibited writers trying to place Ergonomics in a satirical or comedic position and woefully failing.

Nonetheless, the subject is presented on national TV, so fleetingly without continuity it is almost missed. Exhibited in this context, it appears to bring down the public's perception, typical in this genre of television programming.

However, the concept gets at least some attention in areas generally overlooked. The Ergonomics ("humor") appears in the Happy Endings episode S3 EP 04, entitled More Like Stanksgiving (sic) 11/2012.

It seems that without any understanding of the Ergonomics concept the humor has a high probability of falling flat. Scratch that. It completely falls flat.

Here, series star, ditzy Alex (actress Elisha Cuthbert), and co-star Penny (actress Casey Williams) set a table for a dinner party. Alex describes some sort of high-tech "moderne" hanging seating device.

Alex says to Penny: "Brad can sit on the exercise ball, Max can have the camping chair and you can

(hang) here in this **<u>Ergonomic work hammock</u>**,"
No carpal tunnel for this productive gal" lamely
demonstrating its positioning for computer
keyboarding. Clearly mis-understood and obviously
mis-placed.

If it is serious enough subject to poke fun at, then do
a good job, or if it is perceived as fake, then maybe
do a real parody on it. Either way, please do more
than just use it as filler, which virtually no one will
have a chance to appreciate or understand.

The laugh track was even pathetic. But maybe if
one were to evaluate the sit-com in its entirety, it
may be that the writers are so uninformed they
couldn't come up with anything better. But like
Bush II quashing the Ergonomics Law in 2004, he at
least brought the word and concept to the front of
the business section and in some instances on the
smaller newspapers, the front page.

In this way, I thank the writers for doing their small
bit for the profession. I look to mass media
someday taking Ergonomics more seriously instead
of just letting it languish on second rate sit-coms
with laugh tracks.

Such a shame that something important to
someone's life and their pain is shown to be
unimportant or as a subject of feeble humor. Even
the object association selection could use some
improvement. Maybe that's why the series is no
longer available.

# Exotic Car Ergonomics

Many folks are starting to write about Ergonomics and some are quiet good at it. Some super expert writers on various subjects are also seeing the world of Ergonomics creeping into their sandbox.

While it is true that Ergonomics can affect virtually any object, process or method some of these writers brandish the word around with sometimes an unclear vision of its real impact. NOT SO HERE! Following are a couple of great examples of how really great writing can bring meaning to Ergonomic to "everyday" or heretofore unknown applications.

The two following brilliant insights exemplify subjects and viewpoints that are often hidden from normal view to the average reader. These provide a real gift that may have gone heretofore unobserved or completely by passed. This gift enhances the reader's knowledge base to a little known but highly relevant application and shows how it truly affects the human – machine interaction

These are brilliant examples of Exotic Car Ergonomics, or lack thereof, found in media magazine giants, Road & Track Magazine and Car & Driver Magazine. Maybe we should call this Auto Ergonomics - Get it? I didn't think so.

This first example of Auto Ergonomics observations, is one of the best I've read, excerpted from the 5/2013 issue of Car & Driver Magazine.

# CAR & DRIVER

## ASTON MARTIN RAPIDE S

TESTED ⊞ Roars with Gryffindor daring, moves with Slytherin cunning and looks like Kate Beckinsale.
⊟ Ergonomics as cruel as Voldemort, the prisoners of Azkaban have better views out.
*by John Pearley Huffman*

From page 108 – May 2013 Car & Driver Magazine
Author's Collection

## *ERGONOMICS AS CRUEL AS VOLDEMORT,*

WOW!

*"Better views out Azkaban cells."*

*Ouch!...* They must really be bad.

The Aston Martin Rapide S - ©UPTALL / Dreamstime.com

Mr. John Pearley Huffmans' write-up is superb! It makes a car lover salivate and it appears he really understands what Ergonomics really is in the automotive world. My hat is off to Mr. Huffman.

As a sporadic gear head and race car mechanic, I think his take and description on the Ergonomics in the Rapide S is spot on, although I'm only going by the write-up, never having had and probably will never have the opportunity to own, let alone drive one or even sit in one, to verify his observations.

To wit: (the following quote is in the lower right corner of the article's first page)

*"Although the Rapide S has a long 117.7-inch wheelbase - 8.4 inches longer than a Honda Accord sedan's - the door openings are puny and the roof very low. It's easier to get into Kings Cross Platform 9¾ bound*

*for Hogwarts than it is to enter the Rapide with one's dignity intact. **It is an ergonomic wonderland in there too**, with seatbelt anchors sunk down into the seats, seat adjustment controls mounted on the center tunnel and narrow footwells. And it's nearly impossible to see out the back".*

Continuing in the Hogwarts theme, Mr. Huffman's description of the Rapide back seat is:

*"It helps to be an elf if you want to be comfortable in the back seat"*

Mr. Huffman's description and philosophy of the back seat parallels mine, although my view is predicated on limited experience in back seats of pickup trucks, Porsche 911 coupes, Jaguar XKE 2+2 and other semi-affordable or common vehicles.

My personal comment on abbreviated back seats is that the Ergonomics or design involved in them is only applicable to young children or passengers who don't mind smelling their knees for the trip. I find Mr. Huffman's showing the relationship to current pop culture indicates he really understands the nuances of how the subject of Ergonomics relates to the Harry Potter environment, and simply makes me anticipate future articles with the same handling of Ergonomics descriptions.

## *Exotic Auto Ergonomics - Phase II*

OK you motor heads and if you've read this far you really are a motor head or a real Ergonomics fan. Either one, I welcome you to this section of yet another irresistible look at bad Ergonomics.

Following we look at another excellent article uncovered in the Jan 2006 issue of Road and Track. The technical analysis performed by Mr. Gordon Murray is titled Anatomy of a Super Car. The article centers on a Bugatti Veyron 16.4. It is indeed a hot car capable of 250 MPH, requiring you to pull over, insert two separate control keys and go through a pilot's type of checklist if you want to drive over 180. It sports a 16 cylinder engine, probably with atrocious gas mileage, a body made completely out of carbon fiber and a list price hovering around a Million Two. Not the every day commuter car for downtown traffic.

Like most similar articles replete with sexy pictures, the writings make any gear head salivate. But a Million Two? But guess what, according to Mr. Murray for all that cash you get bad Ergonomics.

Here is what a 2012 Bugatti Veyron 16.4 looks like.
I can only imagine what it must be like to drive one
of these.

Bugatti Veyron 16.4
©CHRISNOLAN / Dreamstime.com

Pretty sexy, HUH! Yeah, I would love to have one
too, minus the gas bill, insurance premiums and
maintenance. I would be more than happy to simply
drive one, polish it and evaluate the Ergonomics.

Anyhow back on task, which is looking at the
Ergonomics described by Mr. Murray. Like Mr.
Huffman in steadfastly describing the lack of
Ergonomics in the Aston Martin Rapide, Mr.
Murray takes a similar tact for the Bugatti.

Mr. Murray writes:

> *"The interior is a strange mixture of simple
> sports car and over-the-top luxury, the
> detailing and quality are both fantastic, and
> the tactile side works very well with a
> heavyweight feel to the switchgear.*

### _Ergonomics comes second place to style with several problems with outward vision and controls."_

A Million Two exotic car interior lacking in Ergonomics forethought
Kinda hard to believe!
©PEELER37 / Dreamstime.com

The commonality in both analyses appear to be the profusion of blind spots and the all important usability and clarity of the controls, notwithstanding the aforementioned nuclear power plant.

As for rear vision, I suppose it can be said if you are going 250MPH, you really aren't concerned about what's behind you. Your main concern is probably what's up ahead. Well designed controls like specially configured pedals, shift gates, instrument clusters and contoured steering wheels should help you avoid an approaching cow at that speed.

In looking at the writings of both Mr. Huffman and Mr. Murray, it appears both are in quite agreement with each other and indeed myself. Mr. Huffman places a little more fantasy in his writings as opposed to Mr. Murray, but both appear definitely on target in seriously looking at Ergonomics.

Yeah, I really enjoy their writings and I can even greatly admire both in really looking at what Ergonomics is about in these super cars. Their writings simply make me jealous of their having the opportunity to look at Ergonomics (or lack of) in such exotic machinery and present it to the readerships for evaluation. It is not only the handling of the Ergonomics as subject matter in the articles, but the integration of the other aspects of these super cars, including styling, power train and ride that complete the full descriptions and make me wish I could really afford one. Maybe Hertz or Avis will have a high roller membership program that I can join once I win the lotto. Nothing would make me happier.

I truly acknowledge and pay my respects to both these writers in their technical expertise and also in bringing Ergonomics to an audience in a way that is truly unique and heretofore overlooked. And perhaps in the future, due to these authors, designers will place more importance to Ergonomics.

*Kudos guys! And thanks for the gifts!*

## Chapter II
# State of the Art -
## Elements of Perception

Essentially, few really know what Ergonomics
really is. It currently flies or rather aptly put is
placed under the radar. Most cannot even
pronounce Ergonomist, go ahead and try it. It's
like trying to say TOY BOAT ten times…fast.

Go Ahead - say it out loud, REALLY, REALLY
fast - I dare you!

*TOY BOAT*
*TOY BOAT*
*TOY BOAT*
*TOY BOAT*
*TOY BOAT*
*TOY BOAT*
*TOY BOAT*
*TOY BOAT*
*TOY BOAT*
*TOY BOAT*

Did you stumble? Everyone does. I don't know
anyone who can really do that, although I've never
asked an Auctioneer to try.

The same thing happens with the word
Ergonomist. When introduced in a professional

setting or dinner party, it often comes out "Oh, you're that <u>UHHHH…Ergun, Ergo…</u> Ergonomisisist" or more readily that "Ergonomics Guy" or something else quite clever.

If no one can pronounce it how can anyone even understand it, let alone know what wonderful benefits are hidden within its mysteries? The actual answer is: THEY CAN'T AND DON'T!

*Ergonomics Currently Flies Under the Radar*

**ERGONOMICS**
(under the radar) – get it?

First of all let me say that doing Ergonomics is not just supplying keyboards, mice or under desk keyboard trays or even paging through a Staples catalog and purchasing whatever says Ergonomic on it. A simple upgrade from an old World War II chair to a modern sleek mesh back office chair is also not doing Ergonomics.

Doing Ergonomics is really in a vein of health care. It involves anatomical knowledge of some sort. You can't simply take a 4 hour class at a local community college, read a book or watch a YouTube video and do serious Ergonomics. You simply can't. It is an applied science, just like engineering or information technology. It readily requires education, experience, and lateral thinking among other things. You wouldn't want your BMW worked on by someone who only read a book or took a 4 hour class would you?

It requires application of Newtonian biomechanics along with a proper thought process to address identified pain trigger issues.

Most people don't know this. Most people laugh when you say Ergonomics, asking "Am I holding this coffee cup ergonomically correct?' Yeah! Thanks Dude, like I haven't heard that a million times before.

Most people cannot even FATHOM what Ergonomics can do to improve their lifestyle, ensure their future on their job or keep them doing something they love. Ergonomics affects everything we physically do.

If you don't have pain, you don't need me, you don't need a hotshot Ergonomist. You might be one of those folks who will never get a RMI and you know what? Bless You. Count your lucky stars. But for people doing things, whether its keyboarding, assembling cars, welding up railroad trains or whatever and they develop pain that pulls them from their job, then the best thing they can do is either help themselves with the principles presented in this book or go out and find themselves a competent, real, credentialed and caring Ergonomist. Either ensures they can keep working at their job, supporting their families or to continue doing something they love.

The world substantially has no clue what Ergonomics is, REALLY! Virtually no clue excepting in some isolated circles. The world doesn't know ¾ of what's going on, ½ or even ¼. Like I said they don't have a clue. That really makes me sad.

This cluelessness may in part be due to a broad base of confusion from mis-understanding what Ergonomics can do…and because they don't understand it - may be afraid of it. People don't understand it, people don't know it, people are afraid of it. Corporations are trying to implement "Ergonomic Programs," also a misnomer. A huge level of uncertainty exists.

SEE APPENDIX for a real academic definition.

Confusion is compounded with a bunch of charlatan, voodoo, bad, fake Ergonomists running around giving it a bad name, ruining it for many seasoned, serious and real professionals (see Chapter IV on Snake Oil Salesmen) and those who would benefit from its correct application.

So what makes up all the fear, confusion and uncertainty? In reality, Ergonomics should be readily accepted with open arms. It's really the cavalry coming in many cases. It's help on the way. It can eliminate the source of your pain; it can improve productivity and quality. So why is the word when uttered at a dinner party met with a nodding of the head and your conversation partner says, "Oh, you tell people how to sit". How deflating.

Let's start with explanations of why people are afraid and follow up with real viewpoints of the trials and tribulations that Injured Workers go through when they develop some sort of pain or diagnosable occupational injury.

### Here's why some folks are afraid (of Ergonomics)

There are several reasons for this. One is *mistrust*. How can you embrace something you don't know or understand? This is typical fear of the unknown. Another is *anxiety* because Ergonomics may have just been thrust upon you by the boss. Something complex you have minimal knowledge about. Something to do despite having a 50 hour work week, homework and occasional Saturdays at the plant / office. Some can really get put off and simply feel this is a big intrusion on their busy workday. It is just another thing they have to do to please the boss or fulfill their job description. Ergonomics works best when it's done *WITH PEOPLE* compared with *TO PEOPLE*.

***Fear of change*** is also present, either psychologically or physically. For those who are incapable of change, this specter borders on devastating. Generally it is not change that frightens people the most, it is being changed without their consent that scares them and without knowing what's coming down the pike.

### *First Let's Look at Trust*

The following chart exemplifying many current perceptions was written by Dr. Alan Hedge of Cornell University, considered an expert and pioneer on Ergonomics.

Note his use of the term <u>*Voodoo*</u>. Obviously a noted expert's feelings about charlatans who profess knowledge of and who mis-apply said knowledge to the detriment of hundreds if not thousands of those with occupational injuries.

*Voodoo* brings to mind a shaman witch doctor from darkest Africa or The Caribbean, knowledgeable in dark arts of unholy incantations and magic spells. Someone who scares little kids as well as big kids, convincing believers of their occult powers. However, under the glaring light of truth, analysis, and scientific applications, their mystique falls away and is seen for what it really is, a bunch of smoke, mirrors and intimidation.

Here is Dr. Hedge's mistrust grid / chart showing common perception of Ergonomics verbatim (used with permission of course).

## Voodoo Spells or Sound Science?

|  | *Voodoo Spells* | *Office Ergonomics* |
|---|---|---|
| Strong belief system | Magic | Ergonomics |
| Direct cause-effect beliefs | Yes | Yes |
| Dogma | Established | Growing |
| Power of fear & rumor | Yes | Yes |
| "Expert" practitioner | "Witchdoctor" | "Ergonomist" |
| Practical aid | Dolls | "Ergo products" |
| Practical aid | Spells | "Principles" |
| Success stories | Sporadic | Sporadic |
| Face validity | Poor | Good |
| Predictive validity | Poor | Often poor |
| Confidence in knowledge | Total | Dubious |
| Political clout | Nil | Growing |
| *Scientific content* | Nil | *Often low* |

Yes *Voodoo Ergonomist* falls into this definition, delivering false hope, negligible real effectiveness, and negative impact, often causing more pain than when they started. This chart only identifies office Ergonomics, since most folks are at least familiar with the term in office environs. However, *Voodoo Ergonomics* is also alive and well in industrial workstations. Just look around.

Placed in this type of Franklin "T" or column comparison, it's obvious the *Voodoo Ergonomist* has a lot going for him. However, after careful analysis and review, just like a bad magician, the smoke and mirrors can eventually be seen through exposing just how bad his performance is, based on falsities, taking advantage of his subject audience unawareness.

Dr. Hedge's chart shows faith and belief on "magical" powers are based on false promises under the guise of Ergonomics. It is indeed like witchdoctors relying on fear and blind faith that these *Voodoo Ergonomists* are causing the working world a great deal of harm.

The worst part is that these practitioners are oblivious to it, being terribly self deluded and not having any introspective perspective about what they are doing wrong. Like an arrogant narcisstic witchdoctor who keeps pushing his mantra even though everyone can see through his sham, and unfortunately like a bad smell, they don't go away.

Obviously they are at the pinnacle of self delusion, that he is right and everyone else is wrong and if his way doesn't work, it is the "Gods" of the nether world who are to blame. Essentially it is outright criminal, with their having really bad effects on people's lives and health...***and for that I cannot forgive them.***

### *Let's Look at Anxiety Generation*

Mentioning the word Ergonomics or Ergo program in the context of a company meeting to be assigned to someone, the initial reaction is generally one of "Oh Phooey," more work to do or think about on top of everything else I have to do.

People roll their eyes and give each other a sideways look with Raised Eyebrows. You know, "The Look". It's probably a word completely foreign to them. Maybe they've heard it on late night blue screen TV commercials or maybe have seen it in *erroneous / voodoo* advertising claims. Whatever, they are almost totally unfamiliar with the word and certainly don't really know what it means. Genuine fear of the unknown rears it's ugly head...but if they do make the effort to look the word "Ergonomics" up, the dictionary definition is often presented as a series of misplaced words making very little sense to the lay person resulting in confirmation that their initial instinct to reject the whole idea was completely rational and valid.

Which means general and total unacceptance of the whole idea.

Unfortunately, those who are relegated the task of presenting Ergonomics to others are often those who have either a just a dash of Ergonomics understanding, or those who have expertise in a perceived related field such as safety but have no real potential of contributing significantly to the effort – they've just been assigned the responsibility by a well meaning boss who doesn't understand the concept of Ergonomics, much less what he expects to gain from participation in an exercise of attempting an Ergonomics training or evaluation.

This presenter may be an expert in another but related field including safety, or environmental science or HR, and is seen by his boss to be perfectly capable of implementing a total program, but that is only because his boss doesn't really understand the concept either. It's like telling a joke without a full understanding of the punch line and nuances. How many times have you told a funny story or told a joke with the result of your audiences just going "HUH?" At which time you shrug your shoulders and blurt out "Well I guess you had to be there".

Without full understanding, resources, back-up or experience in the subject and then asked to perform, it's no wonder "stage fright" settles in. Unpreparedness is a direct cause for 'stage fright".

## Minimal Buy-in

This illustrates that without a full understanding, passion and full arsenal to address all the negativity of said audience, the project falls flat, without participation, unless said presenter rides roughshod using whips or threats "if you don't do this and follow directions and fill out this form, you will be docked half a days pay.

Full buy in and participation is almost nonexistent! You know why?

It may be because the audience may feel way down deep inside that they are incompetent and dealing in a subject they are not totally comfortable in. I have seen this manifest itself in many ways. It shows in the lackadaisical implementation of most Ergonomics Programs.

Unless you are paying attention to a specific injury or pain, the general perception is apathetic or a shaking of the head thinking "here we go again", just another "program of the week." It's like moving frozen molasses uphill on a cold day.

# *Let's Look at the Fear Component*

Often plain fear of the unknown is the culprit. I believe it exists simply because no one can see pain. Someone with a bad back gets cards and letters and sad looks when they first slip on the ice, herniates a disk and hobbles around. Everyone becomes immune to this after a couple of weeks or months and they become known as Joe / Jane with a bad back who hobbles around. All sympathy has since disappeared. Anyone new to their circle of contacts may not fully understand, even getting irritated at Joe / Jane getting in the way at the elevator and should simply just suck it up and MOVE! They don't understand, they can't see Joe's / Jane's pain. Out of sight, out of mind (or understanding), seems to be the tune.

There are also several other subtle factors leading to fear, outside of the stick-in-the-mud types who flat out don't want (are scared) to do anything at all.

- They see Ergo being an intrusion without any specific benefit for them – a negative impact on their already overcrowded work day
- They can't see Joe's pain so they shy away from beneficial action

- They think they will have to spend a lot of unpaid time learning a new complex subject and become terrorized they may fail either in public or in private conversation or in an assigned project.
- They don't know what to do with something they can't see.

No one likes to fail and getting someone to become cognizant and competent in a complex science like Ergonomics can be daunting and sometimes paralyzing.

This is perhaps why a massive misunderstanding of Ergonomics exists – it is mistakenly considered to be too complex, too grotesque, too twisted of a science without definitive black or white, only infinite layers of gray twined together with red tape and unthinkable unbelievable expensive costs.

## A Cry for Help (falling on deaf or unknowledgeable ears)

Here's a cry for help, but you have to translate it for understanding. It is simply a conversation with an Injured Worker which doesn't do much to build trust or get folks to believe in Ergonomics.

Following are Actual Excerpts Taken From the Injured Workers Point of View. Believe it or Not, Gleaned From Actual Projects:

"Man, I hurt bad, "I should get something to fix my wrist pain."

"Maybe I'll buy an Ergonomic keyboard or new trackball."

"That didn't work" - "Maybe I'll try another."

"Gee that didn't work either."

"It hurts more" -"Can't keyboard - can't mouse."

"Maybe putting my mouse on the desktop that will straighten out my wrist."

"Wow, now my shoulder hurts."

"Ok, I'll just move it over to the other hand."

"Wonder why my left hand hurts, both are on fire."

"Boss won't go for voice activation."

"Back to maybe a better keyboard or mouse."

"Office manager says that's all we have in the equipment closet."

"I'm going to HR" - "Hi HR I've got pain in my hands and wrists."

"You mean all I need to do is simply pick out a wrist brace from this catalog and I'll be Ok?"

"They're not much help."

"Guess I'll open up a worker comp claim and go to the doctor and physical therapy."

"Doc restricted me from keyboarding and only cleared for light duty."

"Now I have this light duty assembling marketing brochures."

"Picking and handling brochure assembly still hurts my wrists."

"Doc says I can't assemble brochures because my wrists are still inflamed."

"Gotta go tell the boss."

"Boss says sorry about that, but we don't have any other light duty."

"Maybe you can clean the toilets or empty the waste baskets those aren't too difficult to do and you can let your wrists recuperate but we can only offer you that kind of work for 2 hours a day."

"Wow these other light duty tasks still hurt my wrists."

"Gotta go back and tell the boss."

"Boss says "well we don't have any other light duty and if you can't take working here you'll just have to leave."

"I see the writing on the wall and worry."

"What am I going to do?" - "Who's gonna help me?"

Seen time and time again this poor soul can't really believe it's happening to them. I have seen workers cry, holding their hands over their heads to help alleviate the pain, telling me they HATE heir hands. They would give anything to stop hurting and I don't blame them.

Many of these are easy fixes. Some of these are approached too late in the sequence. Some have already had two carpal surgeries or both wrists have been so inflamed for so long it is now a chronic condition that no amount of injections or Physical Therapy or Occupational Therapy or even surgery can bring their pain levels down.

Folks like this are really let down and whatever attempts at Ergo interventions have been done have often been bad. No wonder there is mis-trust and mis-conceptions about Ergonomics.

In cases like these a good Ergonomist, *emphasis on the good*, can at least get the task performance of Injured Worker analyzed. They should be able to at least stabilize the discomfort / pain, not allowing it to increase. In many cases, the Ergonomist can at least bring the pain levels down a notch or two by real awareness training and recommending / providing appropriate equipment, serious appropriate equipment, not just randomly selecting stuff from the Office Max catalog.

With their back injuries, some of these Injured Workers have never even experienced a good fully supportive chair, designed to alleviate their pain…and even if they had a good supportive chair brought to them, they often are not taught how to adjust it – much less given the understanding that it's taken a while for them to develop this pain, that it may take some time before their body adjusts to being in a good postural position. After weeks or months of suffering the injury has increased in severity. With the injury becoming more serious it takes longer to recover, so their impatience turns to condemnation of the solution. Our society has conditioned us to have it our way, have it now, and that the pain and discomfort should immediately disappear never to return.

They hurt in their kitchen table chairs, they hurt at their office workstation chair, they hurt when they go to the movies, they hurt when they go to any restaurant, especially the fast food locales, where chairs are hard, uncomfortable non supportive, and until recently made really uncomfortable to get you out of their restaurant. Now some of these are made moderately comfortable because they figure if you stay in the restaurant you might want to buy something else.

Similarly businesses should take this same approach to keep the worker there and pain free, get them to perform more work and avoid the negative impact of such things like HR time, management time and worker productivity, to name a few.

And make more money in the process.

In looking closely, we have two distinct groups desperately needing Ergonomics, Injured Workers or Workers in Pain and Business Entities, but unfortunately, both for the most part are completely unaware of what the science can do.

In part, this is because we have been bombarded with useless "Ergonomic" things (see back of this book) which even to the lay person are ridiculous. This places subconscious thoughts into their minds that Ergo is really not valuable, but the INJURED WORKERS says "I'll try it anyway". I'll try anything is the mantra. Once tried and failed, the term Ergonomic becomes warranted to belong in the witchdoctor catalog.

Sad to say, the real applications and any real benefit they need is nipped in the bud and most often the Injured Worker never gets any help. This occurs time and time again, followed by the IW sometimes getting lawyer-ed up for future legal shenanigans (see Chapter VI).

Fortunately Injured Workers, who generally don't have a clue, often become fully aware and appreciative only after at least a 10-15 minute explanation, including convincing others to understand what can really help. The optimum 20 second elevator speech about Ergonomics still eludes me.

Education is the key for the end users, but it is hard to compete with such Ergonomic things like Ergonomic rubber bands, Ergonomic potato chips and Ergonomic dog toys. I have been the brunt of many a joke concerning these type of _Voodoo Ergonomic_ things. Like did you design these? Ho Ho Ho – <snicker>,<snicker>.

Do y'all think I'm just talking story? See Chapter VI about a Real Life Case Story, complete with original emails.

♫___ eee ooo ___ ahh
ting tang _____ _____
_____ bang
♫

ooo ___ ooo ___ ___
_____ ____ walla walla
bing ____
♫

©Ross Bagdaserian aka David Seville &
the Chipmunks

# Bad Things That Happen Because of a Voodoo Ergonomist

Another colleague told me of a recent experience. She witnessed an HR professional "promoted" to be in charge of Ergonomics, without any direction, work plan, mission charter, and job description or pay raise. The only known event was her boss one day telling her to take care of any and everything Ergonomic. Apparently, she was really lost.

Additionally, it was not even her full time job. Her idea of Ergonomics was to sit down with the Injured Worker and go through the Office Max catalog or some such and simply ask what kind of wrist brace or whatever item they thought they should have or wanted.

*"Wow – I'll take the blue ones – they match my blue work shirts."*

Forget about needing to determine the actual problem.

It seems many trying to do Ergo (risk managers, safety professionals, EHS types, IT professionals) are stretched so thin they have not bandwidth to make any type of real connection, correlation, correction or care. Shame, Shame.

One would think that there should at least be some creative thought on their part to fix the problem.

But no, it appears they neither have the wherewithal or depth of perception or possibly don't even think or care about the Injured Workers, let alone wanting to do something beneficial for them  Also known as "doing the right thing."

Indeed these people seem to be paralyzed, needing some help without budget or without knowledge. Possibly they still think that a good correction is simply a wrist brace.

They have been jaded into thinking that if something is labeled Ergonomic it has magical powers to heal.  They are almost like a deer in the headlights.  Refer back to the mis-trust chart by Dr. Alan Hedge (p.45) of Cornell University and you can now really see the correlation between Voodoo and Real Ergonomics.

The sad part is that they don't really care about the Injured Worker or that they don't have the concern to understand the overall effects of such lousy treatment.

You wouldn't want a doctor to treat your pain like that would you? The answer is no.  You would fire them and find another, or at the very least see someone else who is you feel is competent and at least can effectively find the source of the problem and then in working with you, articulate a fix.

Every one has been in this situation wherein you have found someone else who can fix a specific malady if your Doctor only says take two aspirin and call me in the morning. Truly you or anyone should not take this kind of voodoo treatment from the person in your company who is somehow misguided and simply assigned the tasking of Ergonomics.

Since we are on the subject, these Voodoo practitioners while some have the best of intentions simply do not have the time or wherewithal to understand the nuances of injury and associated fixes. Yes anyone can practice Ergonomics; some of them even practice GOOD Ergonomics. But truly, for the most part, these Voodooists seem to be doing more harm than good.

## Ergonomist forced-to-be

The scenario goes something like this: Boss to the Safety Manager, Risk Director, HR, or Injured Worker who wants to do Ergonomics:

Boss: OK Joe / Jane go ahead and do Ergonomics since you have a vested interest in it along with safety or risk or helping your other injured friends. The powers that be can't give you much in the way of resources or budget, but here are some Ergonomic catalogs (read office equipment) and you have to bone up on your spare time. We might be able to spring for a couple of classes at the local community college or something, but you have to exercise your creative mind (and I know you have one, otherwise you wouldn't be working here). I know I can count on you, just keep me updated on your Ergonomic activities. Also we would like you to look into an establishing an Ergonomics program.

Oh and by the way you should be able to do this in your spare time. You know what spare time is around here. And yes you will still have to do all the regular chores of a HR, risk and safety manager as well. Good Luck and let me know how it goes

DUH!!

Our hapless assignee doesn't even know where to begin. What's the point? I'm not sure they know how to handle it. Maybe they are just going through the motions with their new title of Ergonomic Specialist. Maybe they are just covering up and hoping no one notices.

Unfortunately, just supplying an "Ergonomic" keyboard or mouse doesn't cut it (remember there is no such thing as an Ergonomic anything).

*However (and this is the bad part) - the Injured Worker won't get cured and will remain injured, and perhaps will even get worse because of the*

***improper application of the "Ergonomic'
devices.*** Such a shame. The worse part is that the
HR Manager (or whoever), feels they have done
the best they can, reporting back to the boss that
there's not much more that we can do. Then the
boss says, well we tried our best, "What else can
we do?" "I dunno". "Well let's see what
happens".

*No real follow up.*

*No real concern.*

Such a lackadaisical attitude makes one wonder if
they really know or even care what they are doing.
You shouldn't wonder…it is pretty obvious.

Let's give them anything Ergonomic and see what
happens? If nothing happens we'll wish for the
best (a lousy plan) then they're pretty much on
their own.

Such short sightedness and lack of compassion
and indeed lack of any real business, let alone
humanistic savvy really has a negative impact on
not only business, and the Injured Worker, but
also on the economy (productivity) and world as a
whole.

# Why Companies Don't Use Ergonomics

Image courtesy of Graphicstock.com

Industries often think Ergonomics is a bad, dangerous or cost encumbering activity without any real benefit, forced upon them by big government bureaucrats making them implement laws requiring them to "take care of workers" thinking they aren't doing enough already.

## 1. They think any type of Ergonomics is going to cost them money

That's the main reason they don't really look at Ergonomics'

## 2. Secondly they are afraid of Ergonomics

## 3. Thirdly they don't understand Ergonomics

Yeah there are productivity activities, called Lean, Kaizan, Kan-Ban and many other productivity activities of the month. In these, a bunch of folks gather around and form small committees to brainstorm what to do for low cost and maximum effectiveness regarding the improvement of productivity, safety, and (oh, my, do we dare say it?) comfort of the worker.

Yeah these work, though 99% of the time there is no real Ergonomist involved. It's like having a committee on brain surgery, having a podiatrist, hand specialist, hip surgeon, heart surgeon, internal medicine specialist and a couple of surgical nurses, but no brain surgeon...unbelievable.

The workers and supervisors go on about what little widget or new tool or method can be installed to improve things, but to redesign elements of a workstation? NAH, AIN'T GONNA HAPPEN. Know why? Because they neither can think in the whole or even in a semi whole picture. The mechanics and supervisor levels aren't accustomed to do that, they only think of maybe trying a new tool configuration, and if it doesn't work it get placed by the wayside and the thought is, that ain't nuthin' can be done or that's just the way it is and to suck it up and just do it because you obviously can't do anything about it and nothing else is available which can positively affect this.

Additionally if the situation is known to affect a shoulder, there should be someone who is proficient about anatomy to lend a hand in understanding what methods can be changed without negatively affecting said anatomical part. Rarely can a mechanic or a supervisor, who are involved in the Kaizan or Kan-Ban events, have the time or expertise to go that deep. This would be the proper time to develop your brain trust! It might cost you a couple of favors, but the input will be invaluable.

Even the high falutin' Lean experts can't do this although they profess to understand the applications; they cannot really do this part.

**Picture this scenario**...Imagine a plywood plant. 4'x8' plywood sheet are visually inspected for defects at the end of the assembly line. Two people stand on opposite sides of the plywood, putty guns in hand, spreading putty on the plywood surface fixing layer defects.

Each one is responsible for half of the plywood – two feet in front of them. One side is a big burly guy with a relaxed attitude, the other side a small wisp of a girl with an OCD complex and intense desire to do well for the company, hardly able to hold the big putty gun. Big burly guy observes that if he misses some defects on his side, the girl reaches over on his side and gets the defect. Supervisor is never around to see this happening. The girl doesn't complain, even when her wrists start hurting... she just does her job (and the other guy's) pulling the company flag. She starts compensating with her elbows to help reduce the pain in her wrists. Her elbows start hurting the next day, so she compensates with her shoulders because her elbows hurt. When she can't hold the gun, much less pull the trigger to dispense the putty, she files a claim because her doctor now says her wrists, elbows, and shoulders all need surgical intervention. The productivity guys were happy because the inspectors at the end of the line did not have to reject any panels until the girl couldn't do both sides of the work.

Business surely cannot continue to think in those terms! If Ergonomics were taught as a productivity tool, this would be different.

Suffice it to say that business doesn't use Ergonomics primarily because they:

- Don't know how
- Can't understand it
- Are afraid of it
- Think it costs instead of makes money
- Had a bad Ergonomics experience
- Can't seem to get anywhere with it

Many in management, say this is the way we've done it and this is the way we will always do it - they don't give a rip about productivity or injuries or employee health. Their head is definitely in the sand. The scenario is different if the topic is saving money. Tell the chief financial officer that you have found a way to cut 5% from the cost of production and they are all ears.

In big back breaking jobs, they will say:

*"That's what God gave you arms for and if you can't take it, maybe you aught not to be working here..... Son"*

They don't care; they don't give a rip, are definitely not progressive and can't laterally think to see the monetary benefits. Bad backs are big bucks.

## So How Do We Address This?

People have to know, or be taught how good it is, good like productivity. However it cannot be at the cost of workers simply becoming faster, stronger, more powerful to make more widgets, working themselves to the bone. Leading to termination because they are so broken down they cannot do anything productive for the company. Like so much flotsam, we'll just let you go and we'll just get some one else to take your place, someone who can keep up the pace, *You Wimp.*

It has to be shown it actually helps. This comes from showing exciting and effective solutions to the masses. Touting how good Ergonomics is and how it can take away peoples pain. It has to be synonymous with pain reduction and productivity, rather than the typical perceived "Oh just another activity that has nothing to do with me", or simply "Just go and pick something out of the Office Max catalog."

Fredrick Taylor made a name for himself in the early 1900's showing companies that there is a scientific method underlying work. His studies on shovel design and breaks showed that working smarter is far more productive than work harder.

Ergonomics has to be presented in a way so it becomes automatic, seamless and uninterrupted. It has to be shown to be totally effective with minimal effort of the worker. It has to include feedback from the worker. None of this "I'm the Ergonomist and I know what's best for you to sit in, whether you are in pain or not" comfort is not the key, pain or non-pain is. None of this frou-frou "are you comfortable" stuff. Likewise the company dictum of "I've been doing this for 30 years and I don't hurt! Wasssamatter with you, you a wimp or something?" has to be addressed.

To be able to do this correctly, a high level of expertise is required, not that of a junior level, or someone who does it part time in addition to their other job. They should be able to converse intellectually and present all the nuances of Ergonomics and to what deep benefits these nuance affect. Mostly a knowledgeable professional should be able to address all the fearful concerns shown by their audience. But most of all, this experienced professional MUST have the skillsets to not only know how to assess the problems by means of a program or otherwise, but they also MUST be able to articulate a solution to any complex problem identified. Even without a design background allowing thinking out-of-the-box, they should AT LEAST be able to articulate a solution, using outside resources, creative thinking, colleagues and naturally by enlisting input from the injured workers. This illustrates to the masses the benefits and thereby become a thing of welcome rather than one of fear.

---

EVERYONE KNOWS AN ENGINEER CAN FIGURE THINGS OUT AND SCIENTIFICALLY SOLVE PROBLEMS (to the benefit of all)

**AN ERGONOMIST SHOULD BE KNOWN FOR THE SAME.**

Ancient Chinese Philosophy

---

Wow, what a set-up for performance anxiety…when Ergo issues often appear in layers like onions – peel one layer back and oh my there's another challenge sitting there… Ergonomics is not a one stop solution, and should not be portrayed to be one; lest the label of failure is assigned to those not solving all the problems with one evaluation.

***I definitely feel you can't call yourself an Ergonomist, at least in the occupational injury arena unless you can offer a solution, a real solution to the serious injury problems.***

A real solution can be defined as a trackable reduction in pain or injuries, shown by the worker(s), a real, not imagined elimination of known and proven at-risk task performance conditions and a happy worker, not one who says, "Yeah, this ergo guy came in and did or said this, but didn't really do much" or "This is what they did and it didn't work worth beans."

No wonder people fear and at the very least are mostly bothered by the subject of Ergonomics. I firmly believe it is partly because they generally don't think it works.

Mostly, Ergonomics is perceived to be a significant interruption and disruption in their professional lives and history has proven with the Voodooists that they often either don't fix the problem or often simply make it worse. I know, I've seen it.

This really pains me to say this about something wonderful, but here it goes.

***The bottom line is this,*** *until someone or something forces a radical change in the overall thinking and perception, Injured Workers stay injured and the spiral keeps going until they can't take it anymore and companies simply continue to throw money away at the problem without real solutions.*

If we continue to conclude that this is an acceptable scenario then:

***SHAME ON US!***

Real ergonomics is viable and does exist (as compared to Santa Claus and talking M&Ms).

I sincerely hope you have it inside you to help change this.

Just think of how many lives you can impact and improve and how many people will benefit from your efforts.

Just think about it.

*Yes, just think about it,* ***Please!***

## So, What is the Global Picture or Current Day State of Ergonomics?

Where do we in the U.S. stand in comparison with everyone else? Currently, the United States is the only country in the developed world where politicians apparently don't think Ergo is worthwhile, at least not to the point of winning re-election points. In various other parts of the world politicians (get this) really do take Ergo seriously, not calling it a voodoo or soft science. They cry out "Yes" we agree with its principles and benefits. Laughingly, many in the U.S. just seem to think it's junk science. Not surprisingly the last thing they say we need is Ergonomics, discrediting the science entirely. Need proof of adverse thinking? Just look at the history of the political in-fighting surrounding the Ergonomic Standards movement back in 2002 (and still currently in play).

Right now there are about 65 Ergonomic ISO standards, and the EU mandates Ergonomics by law in its member countries (as do other countries like Australia and Brazil). Not surprisingly, given the political climate, the U.S. has not really adopted standards to any significant level, especially nationally. It's like we are ostriches with our head in the sand. If we keep avoiding the 800# gorilla in the room we can fool ourselves into the belief that it does not exist and maybe if we wait long enough it will just wander off and we won't have to do anything about it or, even be forced into making some sort of decision. It certainly is a lot easier to leave this guy alone and hope he wanders off by himself and then we wouldn't have to do anything about him, now would we?

We going to do something about this guy?

Or are we going to ignore it?

After all aren't there other more important things than worker health and overall productivity affecting gross national product? We can merrily just keep going along our way and turn our attention towards something really significant, like <fill in the blank with whatever current crisis you favor>.

If you look anywhere in the European communities, 1992 seems about the time they were beginning to introduce Ergonomics standards. Brazil is on record for beginning in 1990.

And wonders of all wonders, even our old "friends" in Iran have an active Ergo program simply to help people in the workplace. They have an Institute of Safety and Workplaces. I don't know of their current activities, since I'm not on their newsletter chain.

But overall it seems the U.S. has a paradox. We are schizophrenic to be sure. Major companies and organizations Poo Poo Ergonomics with other BIG companies touting Ergonomics to be a high-end solution and add-on with marketing their products to seem more appealing, more improved, more *"ergonomic"*. And yet they seem to think they are fooling us.

So there we have it. A real schizophrenic situation about Ergonomics.

**On one hand** companies have determined it to be totally unnecessary, something to avoid, an adversary even.

It is often seen that companies at higher levels don't really respect it, and in many instances go out of their way to down play it saying things like, "We never had an Ergonomic expense before, Why there isn't even a line item for Ergonomics (things). So how could I have an expense on a line item which is non-existent or doesn't even have budgetary concerns? I don't even know that our company ever had an Ergonomic concern. Show me here and now on the ledger sheet where we have problems concerning Ergonomics." They don't get it and they don't understand.

**On the other** hand companies present it as a "value added" marketing ploy, touting wonderful benefits from a product or process. Yeah, talk about a real bi-polar situation. See Appendix listing Ergonomic things that are definitely not, exposing real lies.

Historically, post WWII the discipline of Ergonomics began being a means to improve human performance. It can also be argued that 7-10 years ago every one in the military knew about Human Systems Integration (HSI). This was reportedly a way for these folks to not use the word Ergonomics; they simply rebranded it HSI.

Well, this is one way to avoid using the term Ergonomics; however, if you simply rebrand something and call it something else there is usually a mass of confusion circling the subject, and HSI was no exception. Reflection and regard for the military resulted in this confusion and waffling by politicians.

**What's Happening in Other Parts of the Globe?**

In Britain, The Institute of Ergonomics and Human Factors has now become an intuition, having stringent requirements. These include 5 years application to become a chartered official body with specific activities, bylaws and the like. It follows that those choosing the profession of Ergonomics must follow certain criteria, similar to being called a Physician, noting that you have followed a specific career path with appropriate schooling, experience and OJT and credentialing exams. It pleases me no end to see that the Institute of Ergonomics and Human Factors is a chartered institute, perhaps even having a professional one upmanship of the certifying organizations in the U.S.

The actual term in the UK for an Ergonomics professional is now a Royal Chartered Profession so obviously even the Queen gets it! Unfortunately chartering can't be done in the United States because there is no royalty. Ergonomics is lucky to get lip service for the most part.

## Ergonomics, a Science and an Art

In really dissecting Ergonomics, it closely follows a historical path like many such disciplines trying to accomplish something new or advancing the science. This involves continued analysis, pushing the limitations of current knowledge and often using a "try it and see what happens" followed by "trying something else using the new data gathered (classic design methodology)."

Today to further detail the fragmented science of Ergonomics, it can be said that many Ergonomists are more skilled in one are than another, just like Physicians are often more skilled in one area than another, but all are physicians. It may be said that Ergonomics is pre-scientific like the medical field used to be.

If we again look at history, medicine was definitely pre-scientific in the old days, having its roots in folk medicine with simple cures for relatively simple maladies using things like leeching and bleeding to cure ills.  After many trials and tribulations and inadvertently killing lots of folk, making them worse or at the very least not making the poor patients any better,  practitioners observed, took note, did research determined what did and did not work, and revised their approach.

Hence we now know that medicine is a distinct science in many regards, although the practice is still (with all due respect) sometimes a "hit and miss" still using some form of trial and error.  This is especially obvious when trying to match up a particular medicine in battling some infectious diseases and more predominant in administering psychotropic drugs.  In fact some physicians are still adamant about calling it a practice, and not a totally refined science, of which it will probably never be, because there will always be a condition that requires some sort of experimentation, exploration or "pushing the envelope".

Similarly engineering has the same characteristics in that there are always, even daily instances when engineers are exploring new applications and "pushing he envelope." to try something never done before, trying to expand the knowledge base of successful applications.

Upon further exploration and application medicine and engineering eventually became the sophisticated endeavors we see today. Throughout the ages the practitioners have become more and more scientific with developing the knowledge base, and with these proven techniques and successful treatments, public awareness, trust and acceptance have followed these practitioners to the highly regarded professionals seen today.

The same can be said for whole lot of other professions. Not quite yet for Ergonomics.

It just seems to me that Ergonomists who are often now viewed as voodooists, or alchemists, do not have a great following or wide base of trust in their practice. We still see it today. Sometimes it works and sometimes it doesn't. It seems the science has actually advanced in means of applications and success; however it is the public acceptance that is not quite there yet, maybe because of the short time the subject has been in our collective public consciousness.

Medicine is now a real science and such governing bodies like the AMA ensure its validity and reliability. Even big Pharma also had to change due to the advances. Pulling snake oil (see next chapter on Snake Oil) from the market had to occur. Witness the radioactive suppositories, designed to make you a real man, shown in the next chapter of Snake Oil. What is seen as ludicrous today was probably witnessed as real hi-tech health care back in the day, obviously without public trust and awareness, similar to what Ergonomics experiences to some extent in the States.

In looking at the current state-of-the-art of Ergonomics it appears this discipline is also in the pre scientific stage of development, with a potentially very bright future and also potential big impact on the human task performance.

But only if we do something about it!!!!

In 50 years it will in all likelihood, be advanced to be seen as a highly valuable discipline with applications to almost every man-task or in any instance of anyone doing something, which probably encompasses almost everything, mechanically aided or not.

I look forward to that day, and perhaps you should too for we will all be better off for it.

**Mostly, we should really try and rise above this quagmire of mistrust, bad perceptions and really embrace what Ergonomics is really all about.**

# Just think of all the potential benefits.

## *Chapter III*
# The Snake Oil Ergonomists, Who Lie, Really Lie

It's easy to get fleeced by Voodoo Ergonomists: promising a lot, delivering little, taking your money in the process, causing endless frustration, oftentimes leaving pain in place.

The solution is to determine fakes from real ones by probing into their experience, education, background and work product. You could ask for references and then do your due diligence to see if they really were effective - just don't go on blind faith. This same goes for print ads and products. Look at what they are trying to tell you. *Is it for real or is it just absurd?*

When anyone says or prints Ergonomic this or that and don't back up the claim with authority or research, they're lying - outright lying, the equivalent of saying:

Eat arsenic – It'll make you feel better - Lies

Mostlyscience.com

Theme song for Snake Oilers
(Author's 45 collection)

The olden days had snake oil salesmen touting cure alls for 25 cents. Well, Ergonomic lies are just the same, albeit a lot more, even excruciatingly more expensive. Snake oil purports to save every wrist ache, every back ache, and every shoulder ache. Granted some equipment manufacturers have really good equipment and staff that really knows their stuff, but I'm referring to most media, most paper advertisements, 90% of the stuff on the web and many so-called practitioners.

There are untruths trying to make you believe something so you'll give them your hard earned money instead of the other guy…and for what? A bottle of sweet tasting elixir that doesn't do a thing?

From the movie Little Big Man

> Jack Crabb: *"You don't know when you're licked!"*
> Allardyce T. Meriweather: *"Licked? I'm not licked. I'm, tarred and feathered, that's all."*

I've witnessed it. I've seen it. I've experienced it. I have felt the frustration of those who have been on the short end of such sales and service. The continued pain and pure frustration (often to tears) resulting from this conniving selling false hopes and a real false "Ergonomic" product.

## *Here's a MAGNIFICIENT snake oil example:*

### Vita Radium Suppositories (ca.1930)

Produced by the Home Products Company of Denver, Colorado, these suppositories were guaranteed to contain real radium - and probably did.

From the company's brochure:

**Weak Discouraged Men!**

Now Bubble Over with Joyous Vitality

Through the Use of

Glands and Radium

". . . properly functioning glands make themselves known in a quick, brisk step, mental alertness and the ability to live and love in the fullest sense of the word . . . A man must be in a bad way indeed to sit back and be satisfied without the pleasures that are his birthright! . . . Try them and see what good results you get!"

All Home Product customer orders were shipped in a plain wrapper for confidentiality.

Actual Size
Of Vita Radium

VITA RADIUM SUPPOITORIES, for rectal use by men, are tone restorers of sex and energizers for the entire nervous, glandular and circulatory systems. These Suppositories contain a result-producing amount of highly refined soluble RADIUM, carried in a cocoa butter base. The radium is absorbed thru the walls of the lower colon, enters the blood stream and is carried to all parts of the body - to the weakened organs that need its vitalizing aid. After leaving its durably HEALTHY RESULTS, the radium is gradually eliminated in about three days. Vita Radium Suppositories are guaranteed entirely harmless. Recommended for sexually weak men who, however, should use the NU-MAN Tablets in connection for best results. Also splendid for piles and rectal sores. Try them and see what good results were met.

(Oak Ridge Assoc. of Universities - Historical Instrumentation Collection)

Like these pseudo health enhancers, some Ergo claims are outright scams, false advertising of an inferior product. Some snake oilers actually believe they peddle real positive effects and are really put off, becoming defensive when challenged. They don't back down, try to improve their product or even try to see the light.

The reason? That crass commodity called money, also read ego, causing many a person to cast a blind eye on who they are hoodwinking even to subjects, including religion, advice or Ergonomics.

Now, here's some great *Snake Oil Ergonomics.*

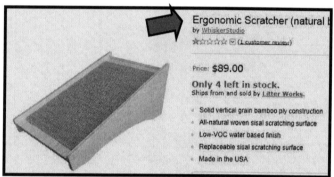

Ergonomic for the cat or owner?
(www.whiskerstuio.com)

Ever seen an Ergonomic stack? Me neither.
(http://www.zdnet.com/15-best-things-to-eat-as-you-tweet_p3-7000002475)

Too often Mr. Snake Oiler awaits in ambush for any unsuspecting soul looking for (sometimes in desperation) a cure, but doesn't understand what they are buying, just going on in blind faith or succumbing to false advertising.

Unfortunately these unsuspecting targets even though bright, highly educated and knowledgeable in the real world, may succumb to Mr. Sleazy, because he the only "expert" coming across their radar. Mr. Sleazy can be very smooth and convincing to the point of really selling their program, methodology or product leading to an exchange of hard earned money for a non existent solution. Of further disgust Mr. Sleazy really believes he is helping someone. How Sad!!!

## This is really disgusting.

The really sad part is that with the wrong workstation modifications, the worker may think it's great, since it might, just might improve the original problem. I have seen workers use a new and different device (chair, mouse, trackball, pliers, wrench, etc.) thinking it is really nice for a little while, only to find out later the pain is worse. So much for Ergonomics.

A black eye for the on-site Ergo, courtesy of Mr. Sleazy. Generally there is no recourse except to try another of Mr. Sleazy's "Ergonomic" things which will undoubtedly have the same effect of

non-working, sorta-working, kinda working or
(and this is serious) making things worse!!

*The well has been poisoned and it will be a while
until someone is willing to go to the well again.*

Not only does a worker in pain get shortchanged,
so does the company.  Unless someone has the
wherewithal to seek some real help the worker
remains at a loss, both injury-wise, income-wise
and otherwise.

## An Ergonomics Snake Oil Case Study

Once there was a technician who blew out both
thumb first knuckles (carpometacarpal joints) by
repeatedly removing specialized testing plugs from
truck radios for over 15 years (see photo).  This
pinch grip was performed at least 15 times per
hour, 120 times per day, 600 times per week,
2,500 times per month, 30,000 times per year.  He
performed this task 15 years, so the math sums up
to right around 460,000 times.  Pretty obvious how
the repetition caused the injury, isn't it?

Once his dominant right hand carpometacarpal
joint deteriorated, he used his left hand and
obviously after a period of time his left hand
deteriorated to the point of a serious worker comp
injury.  Leading us up to part time light duty work,
a diminished paycheck and of course the company

is obviously losing too. How much? Well, that's another long story about the real cost of being injured (see chapter IX - Big Bucks).

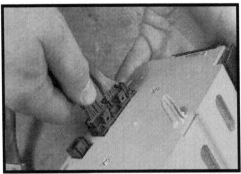

Inserting the plugs / pushing in - no problem

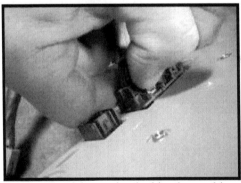

Removing the plug / depressing locking lever - big problem

**Results of Physician Restrictions**

Oftentimes physicians restrict workers, only allowing part time light duty or the new buzz term "modified duty" until either the job of injury is changed or new light duty / modified duty job is found.

In this case, physician restrictions only allowed light duty.

Well guess what. There wasn't enough light duty work to fill up a full forty hours and a 30% pay cut resulted. With years of experience, he is an expert at what he does. The floor supervisors and management really wanted him back to full time job of injury, because this technician was one of the best they ever had, and highly productive

Enter a pseudo Ergonomist. Their thought was that nothing could be done, simply because no specific tool exists to effectively remove the specialized plugs without the damaging repetitive pinch grips. Exit the pseudo Ergonomist. Someone else came in; a plug manufacturer who had "experience" and said he had a special tool which wouldn't cause any pain. Easy in, easy out, was the claim. Assuming that meant for the plug, and not the snake oiler (although maybe applicable to both).

When the tool was trialed, technicians discovered this new 'Ergonomic" tool was just a piece of (baloney), use whatever word you choose. But it was the best the oiler could offer, or the best he knew how and after all he "knew" about Ergonomics, didn't he? At least he said he did.

That's where the project stood. A bottle of snake oil in hand and customers are still ill. No surprise there.

Fortunately, someone in the company had had enough and finally through research, the clouds parted and he was steered in the right direction of serious solution.

Well, advice was given, detective work done, radio & plug samples procured, immediate work commenced on developing a series of tools for the different types / shapes of plugs. The first was made for the main plug eliminating the offending pinch grip, bringing this fellow back down below threshold, allowing him to work again at his original job in spite of injury. The single tool offloaded 80% of the at-risk tasks, and we found technicians could handle the other 20% without discomfort or injury. No other tools needed.

The guy got back to full time duty allowing him to further support his family and a batch of tools was prototyped for the other technicians who were pleased their hands were not in danger. How fun! We even got some wire harnesses for souvenirs.

The following photo sequence illustrates how plug removal was performed with the new tool – complete success!!

1. Place new tool on plug

2. Gently push down to release

3. Gently rock tool -
Careful not to damage plug

4. Plug pops right out

## SUCCESS!!! - NO PINCH GRIP REQUIRED
**Technician returns to work despite injury!**

## *Presenting the DARK Side !*
Specifically for those unaware.

Bad Ergonomics are everywhere because few don't really understand the concept is or what the nuances and consequences are. Be assured there is a lot of bad Ergonomics and it is affecting you, whether you know it or not.

Let's look at those calling themselves Ergonomists who really aren't. Many don't have a problem with someone doing this, because it's usually obvious or should be. Calling oneself a lawyer without passing the bar is an example. Calling yourself a doctor without a med degree is another. However, when one calls themselves an Ergonomist, it may be valid, true and very professional in *their own mind*. After all they may have read a couple of books, taken a class or two and profess they do "Ergonomics", and unfortunately, no one challenges them.

But looking deeper into this, with these charlatans poor work is performed and they think it's OK. Like a serial killer thinking it is OK to do what they do. Science is beginning to uncover genetic links to this propensity. The same might be said for not having any conscience in performing bad Ergo work. The Voodoo Ergos just go along their merry way and continue to do sloppy, often stupid and harmful work.

# Comparisons to Other Life Happenings

Let us take the work of a less than perfect auto mechanic. They may mis-diagnose what's wrong with your car, perform a valve job and charge you a couple grand while you merrily drive off into the sunset. About 10 miles into the sunset you have the same problem and you get a second opinion from a referenced mechanic, with high skills, good experience and a track record of good service. He tells you didn't need a valve job in the first place and that you only needed something simple done, like a thermostat replaced. Try and get your money back from the first mechanic who won't budge. Good luck, you'll see him in small claims court.

Taking it a step further, if the problem was suspension, the shoddy work could have resulted in an accident, injuring or even killing someone (you) or accidentally running some unsuspecting kid over. All because the first mechanic was a cheat and didn't have any conscience about snake oiling.

Potentially a life changing scenario, this charges towards the dark side of life. Think of what could happen with resulting lifelong pain, injury or even death. Frightening isn't it?

Guess What? The same happens with Voodoo Ergonomists. One who is really lightweight and maybe comes from another profession. Furniture salesmen come to mind. I have seen them try and do Ergonomics simply to sell their stuff. What a surprise!

*In this darker side*, really bad work in analysis, problem determination, and solution occurs. Results are harmful and I mean really harmful to the people they are chartered to help.

Three dark things generally happen.

*One*, they absolutely don't do anything to help the poor injured worker, meaning pain escalates or remains high.

*Two*, they can say "Well, this is it and that the way it will always be, so suck it up or change jobs" (a really poor example of people skills).

*Three,* provide a completely wrong and ineffective solution, sometimes paging through an Office Depot or Snap-on Tool catalog and selecting whatever advertisement catches their eye.

# BEST & WORST

WHOA! Granted, there are some in allied professions including Occupational Therapists and Physical Therapists I respect, who do some really good work helping workers alleviate pain and even injury. They fully understand anatomy and nuances of Ergo. **THESE GUYS ARE GOOD!**

Also witnessed is the reverse of OT's, PTs and the like who try and do complex solutions which inevitably fail, backing off thinking that's the best that could be done stating: "That's the way it is injured worker, so buck up", and can't or won't carry the project further to really get it solved. These are the ones unfortunately often permeating the workforce and really doing damage.

Are they really charlatans? Maybe…Maybe not. Maybe they've simply not taken the project far enough to develop a solution. The workers don't get better, are still in pain and often must retire, quit, find light duty or a new job (in my mind unacceptable). Occasionally they lawyer up and go after the employer for compensation for all the physical and psychological pain and suffering.

Unfortunately just like the irresponsible mechanic, the Voodooist can have a negative impact, I mean a really bad negative impact on _your_ life, effecting serious and dangerous events with shoddy work in analysis and solution. Not only will they effectively close the door on getting any real help, by shutting the budget door, but also it may appear you had an assessment and nothing came.

Results? You being the injured worker lose. You may not ever regain the physical ability to perform tasks of your chosen profession and may have to settle for something less, a LOT less. While experiencing constant pain doing ordinary every day things, your interaction with life can be compromised.

**Think about it. Voodooists and Charlatans have the dark power to really do damage to your life. Scary isn't it?**

### _How can you tell a good one from the bad ones?_

This is like any other profession. There are good ones and there are bad ones, but like cabinetmakers, there is no lead-in saying good, bad or maybe even mediocre Ergonomist, just like there is no lead-in is saying good, bad or mediocre cabinetmaker.

So let's take said cabinetmaker for example. Everyone can probably tell a good one from a bad one, simply by the quality of his work (among other attributes). Is he full of braggadocio? Or is he simply confident in his abilities with experience, training and knowledge to back up his claims. Is he professional in his demeanor and does he discuss things appropriately? Does he keep his shop area organized and clean? Most of all does he deliver what he has contracted for or what he says he will do in professional manner? Can you see his past work and (this is most important) talk to his past clients?

Is he passionate and honored to take care of that priceless period piece that's been in the family for hundreds of years? Naturally you wouldn't want just any old cabinetmaker to refinish it, after all it has a lot of history, is museum grade and came with a lot of love history from your grandma.

Or maybe you have that old antique 54 Corvette your uncle willed to you because you shared adventures in it. Naturally you don't want just any old grease monkey to work on it because it's your baby.

Mechanic or cabinetmaker or any other profession, you have something valuable and you can't simply turn it over to "just anyone", even if claiming to be expert. You want friend's recommendations, you want professional references and maybe perhaps you will go and see their previous work. Or maybe they even have a portfolio of past work they will share to give you confidence your "baby" gets the care it deserves.

Well if you don't do your due diligence, you might end up with some piker who'll destroy your period piece, or ruin your classic Corvette doing something obscene to them, even though trying their "best". Their best may turn your baby into a mess, using the wrong finish discoloring the antique walnut destroying the intrinsic value. He could even put in the wrong (but "just as good") engine part making your original equipment dual quad V8 less than perfect and he will tell you that's the best he can do and still take your money.

### *Doing Their "Best"*

Heard time and time again: "They're doing their best" or they have good intentions." Yeah, what are good intentions worth? Especially when messing around with someone's livelihood, health and quality of life, ZERO, ZILCH, NADA!

You want good intentions? I'll show you hollow good intentions.

Let's look at a recent cause-célèbre big breaking story from *http://www.bbc.com/news/world-europe-19349921, - "Spanish Religious Fresco Ruined by Amateur Painter, 23Aug 2012,* which hit the international news.

80 year old Ceclia Giménez simply marched into tiny Santuario de Misericordia church in the town

of Borgia, Spain attempting to "repair" the 19th century fading fresco by Elias Garcia Martinez's "Ecce Homo" (Behold the Man) without permission.

Its one thing to stage a do-it-yourself renovation on a table, mirror or painting found deep in the weeds of a yard sale. But to deface an irreplaceable, if not priceless painting because of "good intentions?" I'm not so sure that's forgivable.

***Good intentions can also screw up your life, now that's definitely not forgivable.***

Let's look further at "good intentions."

Original painting        After "repair" by        Good intentions
                              the restorer                result
*Images from http://www.bbc.com/news/world-europe-19349921*

This obviously has significant impact on church members' beliefs exacting a psychological toll.

A similar physical and psychological impact from lack of foresight and care is forced onto victims of poor Ergonomics. Actually, I admire this 80 year old lady for trying, I admire her fortitude, I admire her need to do this. I am aghast at the final result ruining something that probably cannot be salvaged nor replicated.

I feel the same way about Bad Ergonomists ruining lives. Like this painting, a permanently damaged body due to bad Ergo oftentimes cannot be salvaged or repaired (See P.177).

False promises abound. Everyone has a story of a carpenter from hell found on Craigslist or from a craftsman you found on a bulletin board at Home Depot.

The point is that you have to do a little due diligence to protect your period piece or your 54 Corvette or more pointedly, yourself. If you don't, you can get really burned. Know anyone who has had such a story? We all do.

Well let's take this to a real personal level. Your most valuable possession is not your Paul Revere end table or your 54 Corvette. It is your own body. Your own anatomy. Something priceless, more valuable than any antique furniture piece or classic car - one of a kind (the only one of its kind actually). It could also be the anatomy of a worker you are in charge of, a colleague friend, employee

or someone you are concerned about,
professionally or socially.

  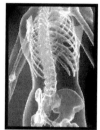

| If you treasure and want to take care of this… | Or you treasure and want to take care of this… | Then you should very well take care of this! |

## Like Diogenes - Looking for an Honest Man / Taking Control

There remains in our midst those who readily
believe they are Ergonomists, and to the chagrin
of all, are doing irreparable harm to the science
and public perception. Mostly they're doing a
disservice to those who depend upon them for
help, who hope they will address their
occupational injuries, symptomologies and help
them reduce their pain so they can return to work
and support their families.

*Okay, okay, hold your horses before you stone me
to death.*

Granted many in the Ergo world (without being
full fledged experienced credentialed

Ergonomists) can do some good work and some of them can do OUTSTANDING work - but like some unknown philosopher once quipped:

*"I've never met a more stupid man than an expert out of his field."*

And believe me; I've seen many out of their field.

Likewise in this nether world of good, bad, mediocre, voodoo, charlatan, expert and wannabee, some do really meaningful work, and often do really outstanding work. Moreover, the truly good ones know when to call in a real expert. Someone who can support them, mentor them through a difficult project and have meaningful impact on an injured or symptomatic worker. They don't give up trying.

Like someone who says he is an expert carpenter, who says he can re-roof your house but his experience is only building dog houses - would you believe him? Yeah, maybe he can do handyman or minor closet to major renovation, but would you trust him to do your roof? He says he can but you know he's experienced only on dog houses. He could even do it half the price of a real roofer. Again, would you have him do your roof? Probably not. If asked his opinion, he should say, if he is a consummate professional:"Yeah, he can build a dynamite doghouse", maybe one that will even win an award on Animal Planet, but he should back off and help you interview and select a real roofer.

Voodooists and Pseudoists don't do that. They put in a keyboard, when it's the chair that's the problem - then unforgivably, they abandon the poor worker to their pain. Some really sloppy "ergo" work is done by those hiding behind a professional moniker. They just don't seem to give a rip.

Several things happen - Ergonomics gets a bad name and ridicule. Company budget is soaked up and there is not much left for a real assessment and everyone starts pointing fingers, especially at the snake oiler. But most of all this wonderful world of real solutions and help has been left with a black eye, a bad rap, and anyone who has seen such a scenario thinks, "Yeah!!, what a soft science or even what a pseudo science." All from a someone selfishly trying to ply a trade they have no real expertise in, save for that 4 hour, $75 Saturday course at the local community college, which incidentally provides a color certificate from their HP printer so "you too can become certified." Hooo Boy!!!

Essentially, they are selling lies for money!

See Alison Heller-Ono article "Deciphering the Alphabet Soup of Ergonomic Credentialing" in Appendix, p.265 on determining proper credentialing.

# A GOOD PRACTITIONER

That's the difference between a Voodooist or Oiler, and those who really have injury prevention, people's future and welfare in their make up. It's in their soul, no matter what they call themselves. They feel purposeful about it. They know when their limitations are met. They may do all they can and maybe even have to readjust their workplan, installations and applications.

Caregiver or Healer might even be an applicable term.

And when at the end of their expertise, they will help you find a more experienced, more creative professional to work with solving the problem. I know some, and I hold them in high regard. **NO, I hold them in REALLY HIGH regard**. Some become professional (and social) friends and have become a valuable part of my life.

*If you find one, hang on to them, because in their heart, they have your well being in mind. Amen!*

## A Challenge

So, if you are in the Ergo trade, I beg and plead with you, get your *passion* up for doing Ergonomics. No matter how seeming insignificant the project.

**A lot of peoples' livelihood and quality of life depends on it and it's up to you to really help them.**

You don't have to be a full fledged Ergo (witness my Friend Joy in Chapter VI - Success Stories) to do this, you just need to care and have a heart and passion to really help someone no matter what you call yourself.

*Otherwise you've got no business calling yourself an Ergonomist or whatever title you use.*

# Stories to
# Help
# &
# Inspire

# Chapter IV
## Psychosocial Ergonomics

*The impossible computer workstation & the impossible worker*

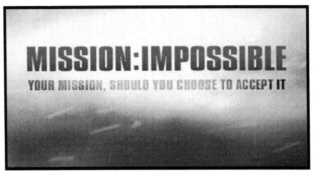

♫ Bum bum bada, Bum bum bada, Bum bum bada,
Bum bum bada, doo de doo doo, de doo doo,
Ba daaaaaaa! ♫

You've run into these impossible types if you are doing anything at all in the ergo realm. If you haven't you will. It's just a matter of time. The old adage states, "Not if, but when."

We've all had or will have bad psychosocial project experiences, begging the question: "Can we fix neck-up stuff or is Psychosocial Ergonomics only about perception?"

"What's with this person? It may be someone who's bit off, maybe a bit eccentric, maybe full blown bi-polar - but it has to do with how they think (or don't think). At any rate their puzzling behavior leaves us dumbstruck in why are they doing what they doing. Clearly they are....well, just a little different. Let's restate that. They are a LOT different. We couldn't live with them, nor can we really call them friends. We try to avoid them whenever possible, and unfortunately, each one of us probably has one of these "different" types for a relative. They are unique in their own right with their circle of friends, loving families and productive lives.

There are, of course some high powered professional firms who deal in behavioral training, using programs attempting to enable workers themselves to take responsibility of their discomfort and hopefully corrections. Some simply can't change, others simply don't want to under any circumstances. Some are resistant to self responsibility. These firms dealing with behavioral change have an uphill battle with difficult folks. Many a story can be had about "battle conditions" faced trying to help someone.

### *The Impossible Computer Workstation Project*

You'll run into these types of "different" individuals sometime, so be prepared. These are the impossible computer workstations, well in reality it is an impossible worker. These are workers that no matter what you do, nothing works.

These types are easily identified. You are generally greeted like this:

"I really don't know why you are doing this, I'm really OK." It's just that "I don't like this, I don't like that, I don't want this, and I don't want that, I just don't like change, I don't even know why they sent you to see me. I don't need any help, I'm really OK."

You cordially reply "I'm here to implement workstation modifications to see if we can alleviate some of your discomfort." "Would you like that?"

"No I'm OK, but if you are going to fix this, just don't change anything."

"What did you say? Did I hear you right?"

"I just don't like change."

"You want me to help reduce your pain."

"Well I've had it for so long I'm just used it and put up with it, I'm fine."

Around and around we go in this circular argument. Further observations result like this:

"I really don't think you should change my mouse," they dictate."

"Well, doesn't it hurt when you use it?"

"Yeah, but I just change hands."

"But doesn't that make the other hand hurt?"

"Yeah but then I change it back again, so it's OK."

"What if we try something different, like a trackball?"

"Nah, I don't want to use a trackball."

"Ever tried a trackball?"

"No, I'd rather use my mouse."

"I thought you said it hurt."

"Yeah, but I'm used to it, it's OK."

***And then, of course, there's this type of impossible client:***

"I don't really want to keep anything that you have done. Nothing works, nothing is right." "It just doesn't work

"Why not?"

"It just doesn't."

Complain, complain, bitch and moan, that's all they do. No matter what you do, how you do it, when you do it, and how effective it is, that's just what they do.

Well, can an Ergonomist really fix these workstation situations or at least get these folks to open up and accept some help? - I ask myself.

Fortunately, I think anyone, a wannabe or havetobe, can do an analysis to the Nth degree and really determine if the issue is purely biomechanical or not.

Maybe you're that good, maybe you're even an expert; learned in the ways of all things Ergonomic to establish a good, albeit modified computer workstation. This is how it generally goes down, and I'm sure any of you Ergo types can really relate to this:

Maybe you've installed the best keyboard. Perhaps it's a high tech model with redistributed and relocated keys addressing such oversights by those who first designed the keyboard in the 1870's. Maybe it takes care of wrist bend placing it in the most body neutral posture you can think of. Maybe it is tilted at just the right angle to eliminate any wrist flexion and extension.

You've also thrown in all known off-the-shelf high tech input devices. You've used, specialized laser activated things offloading the <tab>, <esc> for the left hand pinkie which forces adverse positioning or offloaded the dreaded, right hand pinkie <enter>, and <back space> keys.

Now that you've put in the appropriate under desk keyboard tray, input device, choosing pedals, digitizing tablets, joysticks, foot mouse, input stylus, finger mouse, air mouse, forehead laser mouse or any creative thing you can source for computer input, you turn your attention to the chair.

What about the chair?

By now you've put in a highly adjustable (almost custom) chair, the seat pan specifically fitting the derriere in question. Large or small, wide or slim, height/weight/proportional (HWP) or non HWP, it has appropriate clearance behind the knee (popliteal crease) allowing the user, whatever shape they are in to put their butt way back in the seat. This allows full contact with the chair back without the front of the seat pan hitting them in the back of the knees (inadvertently forcing them to sit on the front edge of the chair). This little detail is incidentally a main back pain trigger. They simply sit on the front edge of the chair without any back support, in static loading all day. No wonder they hurt.

As for the chair back, you have undoubtedly installed the most appropriately contoured back, that tilts independent of the seat pan, goes up and down easily (and I mean easily) and has a blow up whoopee cushion (really called an inflatable lumbar support). Like the seat pan, the back should be specifically sized out fitting the user.

Those who are a bit on the heavy side should get a wider back. Those who are on the slimmer side should get a contoured back which has "wings" to wrap around for full rib cage support

Perhaps you've made custom armrests with platform extension allowing split keyboards to be placed on them, keeping the upper arms vertical, relaxing the shoulder musculature removing all stressors here and in the neck, and totally eliminating inward arm rotation seen with typical keyboards. This is especially useful for those who have an exceptionally large body mass & girth, being in the super heavyweight class.

*At last*, you've installed the best, best, best workstation money can buy and your creative intellect can design, with special items addressing all known symptomologies of your injured worker.

At this point you've tried everything you know how for computer workstation solutions. You have also explored their personal activities including ADLs, hobbies, recreation. Nope, they don't do anything except eat frozen TV dinners slouching on the couch watching the tube.

No pets, no hobbies, no relationships, no outside activities.

"I rent a lot of movies", they say.

So, bottom line, still they complain, and complain, and complain, and complain.

So what is going on with these can't be fixed types?

Well, by now, with your ingenious workstation modifications, you've fixed all their biomechanical problems and symptomologies, installing special equipment and made from space age materials custom devices. Maybe you even had special cushions built for their derriere (I know, I've done it). With all your education, experience, creative soul, including tapping into every trusted colleague, picking their brains, you still get nothing but complaints.

In case you are wondering, yes, this was a real case assignment, without any benefit of forewarning. I did my best and this worker turned into a raging nightmare that wouldn't settle down. They wouldn't accept anything in any which-way at all…a stone wall refusal on all fronts.

After multiple trials, humiliation, disgrace and loss of face settled in, along with deflation, tail between the legs kind of thing - it was embarrassing. I literally hung my head in shame. None of my training in biomechanics, anatomy, design or Ergonomics had ever given me a glimmer of hope in how to deal with such a stubborn and impossible human being. Having run out of options, I didn't know what to do. Everything I said and did was rudely and effectively rebuffed.

Management knew the difficulties of this person and they were (secretly) hoping I could appease her and shut her up because her attitude impacted co-workers, and their productivity. She was always complaining about her pain and how much her keyboard and mouse were the bane of her existence. Management was tired of hearing this. Adding to the drama, she would often walk into Human Resources office, complaining about her pain to the point of tears using the HR manager as a substitute therapist.

I walked into this project, wide eyed and naïve, thinking pieces would eventually fall into place once I had gone through my toolbox. NO WAY! I was simply a pawn, a hired gun brought in to eliminate a problem. I tried my best. I tried to coerce this young lady by touting benefits. My efforts fell on deaf ears. I tried to show her why these things would work. Rejected. I tried to sweet talk her using all the charm and justification I could muster. Nothing positive. I was at a dead end and there did not seem much I could do about it other than turn tail and admit defeat.

In admitting defeat, I found the light and discovered this is really psychosocial in nature and not biomechanical. Being an expert in biomechanical stuff, does not prepare you with a skillset to deal with psychosocial stuff. Neck down Ergonomics, vs. Neck up Ergonomics. Plus, I'm not really so sure there is neck up Ergonomics other than dealing with cognitive elements in the Human Factors realm. At any rate I found out very painfully, that I was completely unequivocally unable, by training, skill set, intelligence, or persona to cope with this type of Psychosocial Ergonomics - which has everything to do with angle and perspective, impression and the sense of reality.

Round and round we go until we can either convince her by sheer logic or by management mandate to work with the modifications. And GUESS WHAT? Lo and Behold, they begrudgingly accept a few modifications, but still use the mouse, are still accepting the pain, which will undoubtedly become chronic and she gives no further valid reason to do anything different.

At this point management pushed me into a path I had never tread before.

They asked me to document *In Minute Detail* what modifications were installed, along with justification all the way through detailed biomechanics, medical reports, pain patterns and medical history. The final closing report, on my end, was to include my overall opinion and observations on whether the modifications should work irrespective of whether the worker wanted to use them or not. This is how the closing report ended.

*"It is my objective opinion that the workstation modifications have addressed all the biomechanical issues uncovered in the original analysis. However, it appears the worker neither desires nor will accept any such modifications to completely address existing injury / symptomology patterns."*

*"If the installed modifications or new equipment are not used, symptomologies will undoubtedly continue, having a high probability of becoming chronic and potentially debilitating."*

Case closed, after long last the finish line is reached! Turns out, it was definitely psychosocial in nature, and absolutely positively political in reality.

Management then would use this (before & after workstation / biomechanical action, and modification designs / drawings) detailed information, placing it in her personnel file, ready for the time an ambulance chasing attorney might show up at the door making trouble, indicating the company "crippled her for life."

To quote a famous rock band, The Eagles: "The more I think about it, Ole Billy was right, let's shoot all the lawyers, let's shoot 'em tonight." From their

hit Get Over It, Referencing William Shakespeare
from Henry VI, Part 2.

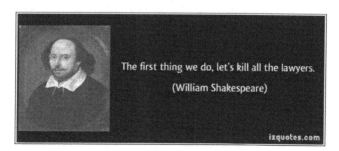

In this particular case Ergonomics became a defense
mechanism in preparation for any potential legal
action from a hostile or belligerent worker who has
perceived wrongs against them. It seems strange
doesn't it?

However, the company rests on the notion that they
have done everything - absolutely everything -
possible to alleviate the worker of their stated pain
and suffering… and the courts will undoubtedly rule
that the company has done their due diligence in
performing every possible reasonable
accommodation to permit the worker to perform
their tasks, no matter how heinous those tasks are
perceived by said worker… or at least that's what
the company is hoping for.

Amazingly, since this project, I have been retained
to perform similar assignments. Maybe Ergonomics
is delving into new and uncharted waters.

AND YET, ON THE *UPSIDE* OF THIS
PSYCHOSOCIAL CATEGORY, THERE'S MORE,

This impossible worker story begins with my colleague, who has no problem, even outwardly enjoying relating it to me:

> *"They complain all day about all the things we've done for them."*

Sound familiar?

My colleague, a high level EHS manager in a really big company, PhD level, a heart of gold, is tough as nails when it comes to compliance and safety. Her philosophy is:

> *"I'm not here to make friends; I'm here to get things done."*

She once told me that one of her biggest problems was "menopausal" women (***her words, not mine***), irrespective of ethnic background, economic position, class of upbringing, education, personality, physical attributes, eye color, hair color, or whatever, have a high probability of getting symptomologies by osmosis.

"What??? Osmosis," I laughed.

My colleague says this is reality, and that she sees this A LOT! She says after solving all discomfort issues by the best, most well trained, professional, these "menopausal" women still have symptomologies.

My PhD friend tells me this complaining is contagious. Not just one or two others saying "Yeah, she has (fill in the blank) and now that you mention it I have the same thing."

I can only liken it to male pregnancy. Just ask the guys who have sympathetic weight gain and emotional distress during their wives' pregnancies. I know what that's like, I had it. I don't know where it came from or what caused it, but I was one of the worst pregnant fathers that ever walked the earth. My young bride wondered who was this guy from Mars (like the book). Psychosocial (perhaps). Physical reaction (conceivably). Hypochondriac (maybe). Deluded and misplaced health anxiety (possibly).

In short were my symptomologies real (maybe, maybe not)? But something similar may be happening here.

For my friend, no more workstation tweaking, all modifications complete and appropriate. Further analysis cannot determine what is wrong.

What to do? What to do?

After all the workstation modifications my friend started thinking out-of-the-box, figuring maybe their problem was not TOTALLY biomechanical, but maybe had psychosocial implications.

Fortunately, in her out-of-the-box thinking, my colleague found a Chinese acupuncturist who moved to the US for further medical training, and had been doing acupuncture since he was four. Being head of neurosurgery back in the mainland he knew his neural tracks.

At a professional conference, my colleague listened to his presentation saying acupuncture can work for some and not for others. He boldly stated that within a 20 minute interview he could tell whether it will work or not on any individual.

The gauntlet was thrown. Would this work for the impossible "menopausal" women?

My colleague let the women know of this character. The ringleader went for the 20 minute interview. Results were positive; the acupuncturist said "yes I can help you." Subsequent appointments were made and attended under company policy.

Guess what? After two months the woman was symptom free. She was so elated she informed her friends and anyone else who would listen.

This woman has subsequently gotten many in the "menopausal" group to go to the acupuncturist and at last report, some departments have settled down to the point wherein work station modifications addressing actual biomechancial issues are having a real positive effect. Accurately predicted by the acupuncturist, it didn't work for everyone, but faith works wonders and it did work for a bunch of them.

My friend couldn't stop giggling when she told me this.

The point here is that a real analysis and correction can and should address any purely *biomechanical* issue and if all paths are taken there should be no real reason for pain or symptomology (given current medical diagnosis, pre-existing conditions and such). If this is not the case, then there may indeed be answers which impact Ergonomics, but are definitely not Ergonomic in themselves, perhaps residing in alternative physical or metal health care areas.

**The theme here is not to stop if a solution is not readily apparent.**

Keep trying (classical design methodology). There's too much "Yeah try this Office Depot Ergonomic chair and if that doesn't work try the other one at Staples." This loop goes to ad infinitum all the way to Shari's Used Office Furniture, with a slogan of "We have everything you'll ever need for an office." Such short sighted thinking exists today. If the answer is not immediately or easily found, everyone gives up. Please don't, for your sake and for the sake of the workers in pain desperately in need of assistance.

Understand this is not about alternative healthcare modalities themselves, but the frustration the workers who are in pain realize. Without an accustomed sense of immediate pain reduction, frustration continues often without a solution apparently available.

Thus the overriding process should illustrate that workstation modifications are first needed to address pain triggers; sometimes followed by a secondary element (alternative physical or mental treatment) to make the workstation modifications work.

Without a methodical sequence of events, first fixing the workstation and then applying secondary approaches, workers may well return to a pain inducing workstation even after visiting someone like our acupuncturist.

Whether this type of thing is biomechanical or psychosocial, who cares? It works effectively, it shouldn't matter if it involves crystal balls or tea leaves, but the caveat is, IT HAS TO WORK!

This holistic approach can be very effective and sometimes they work so well, they make you laugh in wonder. I only wish more practitioners like my colleague (who incidentally keeps saying she is not an Ergonomist) would realize this and not just be caught in the Ergonomic this or Ergonomic that loop without really solving the problem.

**Big Kudos to her** for having an open mind and lateral thinking to actually solving the problem, at least for some folks. Could it be simply a placebo effect, wherein any exotic oriental mystic or shaman who can wave horse tails over the painful areas, burn incense and chant unrecognizable chants works? If something is successful, and it doesn't hurt, why not keep doing it. Was it psychosocial or biomechanical? Who can say, but you sure can't argue with success.

YOUNG GRASSHOPPER, know this:

*When you see such surrender, complexity and short sightedness, a direct path to success is difficult. Care of the body must precede care of the mind before any alternative way can truly be effective.*

More Ancient Chinese Philosophy

*Overall Conclusion*

*This whole set of experiences still raises the question of whether there is or isn't such a thing as Psychosocial Ergonomics*. In fact it sometimes appears to be somewhat close to an oxymoron, with Ergonomics still dealing in the realm of task performance (someone physically doing something). Thinking or meditating does not seem to qualify as Ergonomic sport.

The workstation modifications here eliminated the pure biomechanical triggers, allowing a secondary approach (acupuncture) to remain effective, rather than letting these women return to a bad workstation to develop symptomologies all over again.

*Like I said: "You can't argue with success!"*

---

## *HOWEVER, LET'S GO ON TO THE EASY FIX*

In keeping with the psychosocial theme, there exist many who think Ergonomics borders on the magic pill bandwagon. Like a firm disbelief system fed by fear, awe, mystery and general ignorance (see Dr. Alan Hedge's Voodoo Ergonomics in Chapter III, State of the Art , page 45), many believe simple cures should be available, in the form of pills  Once easily taken, all will be amazingly well.

Well, I'VE DISCOVERED SOMETHING AND IT'S NOTHING NEW

Everyone wants an easy fix.

**Following is yet another type of impossible project person who is not open to solutions and only pays lip service to any approach.  "I want what I want when I want it, the way I want it."**

Here we have the Ergo pill.  What is it?  Well, what do you want it to be?

## It is what it is when it needs to be what you want it to be.

This looks to be a common refusal of help. We find this prevalent attitude is alive and well, not only with computer workers, but also in the trades (it's everywhere, it's everywhere). They feel this is the way we've done it, this is how we do it and this is the way we'll always do it, pain or no pain.

They say:

> *"That's what your maker you arms for and if you can't carry this here heavy weight all day, then maybe you ought not to be workin' here!"*

Gee, do you think they can embrace change? Maybe they're too stupid, NAH. Maybe, they're incapable of change, NAH. It simply appears they're just scared to change, possibly just too lazy. I don't know why, but maybe it's the exact same reason, our afore mentioned young lady refused to change. Denial works when all else fails.

> *If it's an easy fix within a couple of minutes and doesn't require any effort on my part, maybe I'll give it a try - maybe you just need some castor oil.*

Too inflexible, too scared, too lazy, maybe so or maybe just in too much pain. Fear of the unknown, panic attacks, fear of change, and fear of failure.

My father had this problem. Too scared, also showing itself as being too stubborn. Like all fathers, minor medical issues surfaced in his senior years. He had a fondness for shrimp, who doesn't? Unfortunately this fondness resulted in painful foot gout. Time and time again he would eat shrimp, develop painful gout and go to the doctor for treatment and pills. Time and time again he would wait, and wait, and wait, until the foot pain became intolerable. Often simple bed sheet weight on his feet created so much pain, he couldn't sleep. Talk about waking up grumpy.

Time and time again he would repeat this eat shrimp, wait until unbearable pain until even entertaining the thought of a "possible" doctor visit. When pain became so bad he couldn't walk, I had to forcibly drag him out of the house in a wheelchair, and at the doctor's office, the receptionist physically pulled Dad out of the car to get him seen.

Maybe, he just wanted to delude himself that someday he would wake up and it would be gone. The more I work with workers in pain I find the older generation has a significant resistance to helpful change, The X or Y generations, not so much probably because the world is changing so fast. Thanks in large part to the technology pace with information overload and such.

For a large portion of generations past, the attitude seems to be just tough it out as long as you can and then maybe you can ask for help without looking like a wimp.

To this end, some stubborn types want convenience (fix my pain NOW) without being bothered by complex health care. A lot of the X & Y generation welcomes me with open arms. "Man, am I glad to see you. Please take care of this so I can get back to work." It's not "Get outta my face, leave me in pain and let me get back to work," but "take care of my pain so I can work healthier, faster and without being distracted." It's like not wanting to "tough it out" nor having to work while having a nagging toothache.

The older generations' machoism seems to exhibit the attitude shown by Jesse Ventura, in Arnold Schwarzenegger's action movie, Predator (circa 1987) where Poncho (actor Richard Chavez) observes Ventura (playing the part of Sgt Blain Cooper) saying:

*"You're hit, you're bleeding."*

To which Sgt. Blain (Ventura) replies with a big glob of chew in his mouth:

*"I ain't got time to bleed."*

©KERENGOL / Dreamstime.com

In a scene taken from the movie Predator,
Sgt. Blain (Ventura) complete with a
mouthful of chew saying:
*"I ain't got time to bleed"*

Just like my Dad and a lot of other trades workers,
"I don't have time (care) to take care of my pain.
I'll just let it go until I am permanently disabled."

Of course unless there is an easy, a *really* easy way
out.

And that way out is naturally an easily swallowed
pill. We all love pills. We are conditioned to take
them to cure almost anything. Getcha up, getcha
down, getcha high, getcha low, getcha so stoned,
you can't even feel the pain or maybe get you so
stoned you won't care you have pain. You won't be
able to work either, but that's another story.

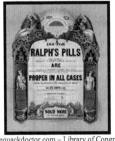

Thequackdoctor.com – Library of Congress

Image courtesy Clker.com

We are a society addicted to pills in one form or another, vitamins, sleep aids, gas, pain relievers, whatever. So, why not for occupational injury? Some simply want a magic pill to cure their ills. Just take two of these and your back, neck, arm numbness, pain or tingling will go away without any effort on your part.

Well guess what? You do have to do something and that simply is to try something different, with proper guidance of course.

Maybe we could re-introduce the old smart pills (M&Ms labeled with the word SMART on them). They were a big seller out of joke shops in the 60s. We also called M&Ms *attitude adjusters*.

Never mind calling anything Ergonomic or not, just a little Brother Love's Medicine and you'll be fine. The equipment or different way of doing something had nothing to do with it. It's just like what Ergonomics was once thought of, smoke and mirrors. So, there really isn't an Ergonomic anything. It's really hocus pocus combined with a little placebo, RIGHT?........RIIIIGGGHTTT.

There appears an Ergonomic everything else from coffee cups to carpet to pens to chairs, to curling irons, to toilet seats to 100's of other things. In this light we could sell Ergonomic pills, which would naturally conform to the shape of the esophagus.

We could even simply use M&M's with the word ERGO stamped on them and no one would know. After all, chocolate is known to be a cure for a lot of things, including depression…so why not? After all Chocolate is also known for relaxing the cardiovascular walls…so it can be taken for prevention of a cardiovascular event.

An anti-stubborn pill would work with our resistant workers (or my Dad). An open mind pill (perhaps just an empty capsule) would also help. A pill for all that ails you and if an occupational injury is your problem, these will work wonders. Maybe label them according to professions like plumber, gardener, accountant, doctor, programmer, etc. I betcha you would feel better, and if you don't, just double the dosage and supplant with some good red wine. Now that should really reduce your symptomology.

> "Here, just take two of these and don't forget to use that new fangled Ergonomic thingie…you never know if it might help or not…and call me in the morning!

Ahhh, if only this were true! Then maybe, just maybe we could say with conviction:

***IT SEEMS THERE REALLY IS SUCH A THING CALLED PSYCHOSOCIAL ERGONOMICS!!!***

# One Last Story
### A Trade Secret Solution for the True-blue Worker

Staying with the neck up (psychosocial) aspects of Ergonomics, presented here is a project involving a lovely lady, a wonderful personality, good sense of humor and smart as all get out. A transfer from Washington DC, graduating from a fancy Eastern university and worked in law offices. Really knew her stuff.

Her main job was to oversee policies of a major municipality. Her specialty included enacted laws and legislation, reading and editing stuff that makes most peoples heads spin. She's an avid reader, reading probably one book a week and just LOVED to read laws and policies making sure they're correct. She also LOVED her job. Perhaps she loved it too much. A true-blue worker, you know the type.

She's constantly keyboarding and mousing, researching intricate things on the web concerning the latest on lawmaking, high level policies and integrating findings and policy making with the local jurisdictions. Naturally, being so "into" her work, 50-60 hour, sometimes more, work weeks were common. She also works after dinner on her home computer. Many weekends find her at the office. Workaholic seemed an appropriate term.

She was apparently drawn by an inner fire to this type of work, relating to it with passion on a level rarely seen. She had it in her to go above and beyond the call of duty showing the "boss" how good or indispensable she really is. On top of that she was burdened by hellacious deadlines to get certain things done. She would complete four day deadlines which would normally require six. Hence heavy workload and projects kept coming and coming and coming, triggered mostly by unending political activity. Oh yes, motivation also included a healthy fear of not wanting to lose her job.

As you may have guessed, medical diagnosis was bilateral carpal tunnel syndrome and tendinitis. Her wrists and hands were always on fire. That was my assignment. Oh, by the way, the Attending Physician's dictum required a break from keyboarding 5 minutes every hour.

This seems plausible doesn't it? A previous attempt of implementing breaks was an egg timer. Whenever the alarm sounded, she was to simply take a break and reset it. Now that's real Ergonomic isn't it? Well there are exactly **TWO** chances of our young lady adhering to this regimen using an "Ergonomic" timer knowing her propensity for working at a breakneck pace.

## *<u>Slim and Fat!!!!!</u>*

Psychological stubbornness, work dedication, fear or over zealousness?  Answer: unknown or simply undetermined.

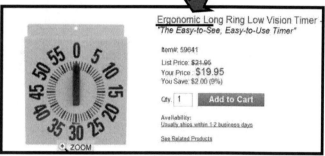

Ergonomic Long Ring Low Vision Timer -
"The Easy-to-See, Easy-to-Use Timer"

Item#: 59641

List Price: $21.95
Your Price : $19.95
You Save: $2.00 (9%)

Qty. 1    Add to Cart

Availability:
Usually ships within 1-2 business days

See Related Products

www.rehabmart.com

The next trial was a simple alarm clock - same result, except the snooze alarm was continually hit until it timed out.  Keyboarding didn't even slow down except for time necessary to hit the snooze button.

Then came computer programs or apps automatically popping up some cutesy thing on screen overriding your work exclaiming "It's Time to Take a Break Sweetie."  Overriding these types of programs elicits the identical snooze button action, just hit any key.

She simply could not or would not let anything get in her way when she had a deadline looming.  Management sided with the doctor really wanting healthy wrists.  After all, she is a valuable employee, but was taking more and more time off due to the hand pain.  She even missed our first intake meeting, calling in after I had already departed from the office to see her.

For some reason, pride in her work, passion for her work, her sense of duty to the job, to her boss to those who depended on her, or a fear of job loss, prevented taking physician mandated hourly breaks. You would think her pain would be motivation enough. But in all my experience, I have witnessed that like money, pain is not necessarily a motivator, at least for the long term.

This was how the project was presented.

After the detailed analysis and workstation modifications addressing her wrist problems were completed, the 5 minute break issue was confronted. Fortunately the other modifications went in seamlessly but this last subject was beginning to make me sweat bullets. Short of standing behind her and removing the keyboard, telling her to do something else every 55 minutes, I didn't have a clue.

In researching computer break programs, I notice some simply blank the screen for the allotted time or provide cutesy exercise graphics. Their downfall is like your snooze alarm in the morning. I can keep reaching over and shutting it off ad infinitum. Our young lady can do the same. Besides, who has time to voluntarily stop and stretch? "Certainly not me." "I have important work to do." "I have imminent deadlines." "I have to keep my job." All reasons for hitting the snooze button.

But what if we install a program without a snooze button? What if we install a device that doesn't even have a snooze button? Now that sounds like a plan!

Well, in thinking of different shut off devices, what are the alternatives? Can the keyboard be shut off? Maybe, probably frustrating, since it might take her awhile to determine that keystrokes weren't working and work might be lost. I sometimes write without looking at the monitor, only looking at the keyboard and thinking / writing at the same time. Incidentally, I am doing that now. If I looked up and found out my last 30 lines were gone, I would be highly irritated. Being sometimes an original thinker I don't know if I could easily get those thoughts back. She might be the same.

Turn off the computer? Same problem along with the additional chore of having to reboot.

What if only the monitor were turned off? Well then, the computer would still function and keystrokes would still be recorded, however you just couldn't see the screen, all else would be unaffected.

So research was done and a device procured, a 110 volt plug-in programmable timer that received the monitor plug, and then itself plugged into a power strip or the wall. It has 75 timing events per 24 hour period, more than sufficient for an 8 hour day.

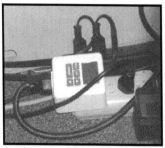

| | |
|---|---|
| Leviton programmable timer – note override button – about $75 | Timer installed *way* under desk, on the floor, in a power bar way back discouraging snooze or override shut off |

With management permission, the monitor was programmed to come on at 7:45 am, in case she showed up early, with appropriate 5 minute breaks (AKA monitor off events) throughout the day until 5:15, when the monitor was off for the night. It was even programmed to be off all weekend. Couldn't program holidays though, the timer isn't THAT sophisticated. It took roughly 1 hour to program the thing with about a 1 hour familiarity session along with several calls to tech support. It was much harder than programming your DISH TV DVD recorder. It was also very boring and frustrating. Most of us can relate to that with a new fangled electronic device having horrible directions in teeny tiny print, written in bad English.

Like every other break software or alarm clock, it has an override (button). However, this particular bit of information was clandestinely withheld from her. The timer was plugged into her power strip under the desk knowing she wouldn't have dexterity or desire to crawl with hands and knees on the floor reaching way back to override every 55 minutes. Pure Genius, don't you think? Ho Ho!

At last report, management was taking a serious look at workloads thinking about hiring some help to alleviate the long hours and wrist damage to her wrists. So a complete solution is coming addressing facts uncovered by the Ergonomics analysis. What a win-win using pure methods, addressing Psychosocial Ergonomics.

## A Final Note to All You Ergo Types Out There

These "psychosocial" elements are things you never think about in Ergonomics School. These are the things you are totally unprepared for when you enter the real world. These are the things that really test your mettle, forcing lateral thinking.

Are you ready for these kinds of challenges? I hope so, because you'll find yourself in the middle of one sooner or later, and when you get one, let me know, I would love to hear about how you implemented your solution.

# Chapter V

## How to Solve a Complex Ergo Problem

*To really solve injury problems, you **MUST** provide a real, working solution. To develop solutions, you require an intimate understanding of the problem. Not simply making Office Max recommendations.*

Ever read detective stories, or watch CSI shows on TV? The Sam Spades or Charlie Chans of the world? Ever been amazed at how they determine the cause of murders and find the bad guys through diligent detective leg work?

Take some techniques and advice from this guy and his brethren...minus the cigarette

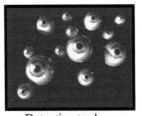

Detective tools
Image courtesy of Graphicsstock.com

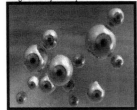

Ergo tools
Image courtesy of Graphicsstock.com

Detectives look at a result, usually murder and put together clues on how the crime occurred, all the way from the smallest detail (microscopic debris) to large obvious causal relationships.

They look for anything that would have relationships to the result (dead body). Similarly good Ergonomists should look at anything related to the medical diagnosis or injury. Without specific diagnoses, digging is needed to determine causal relationships to discomfort or pain. Sometimes it's easy; sometimes it's hard, requiring an open mind and sharp eyes, oftentimes using severe detail oriented lateral thinking, just like detectives.

To be a good Ergonomist, you must be just like one of those TV or real life detectives. If you've ever hung around a police station, interacting with these guys and gals, you know what I'm talking about.

Image courtesy of Graphicstock.com

Sometimes it isn't just forward lean causing back ache. Sometimes back ache doesn't have a forward lean component. Once we found a mammogram technician who had a severe backache.
You know what the problem was? With every mammogram, she tilted her head for a better viewing angle. She didn't take a scoliotic, lordotic or kyphotic back posture, but she did pull her right leg back like a track star in a sprinters stance. Not knowing why she did it; she just did it, each and every mammogram. In studying this particular posture, it appeared to subtly shift her sacral posture relative to her vertebral column (quadratus lumborum / spinal erector musculature site).

The point here, like detectives, the approach (alternate posture trial) was based on a solid knowledge base, observation, and just plain noodling (thinking of other possibilities / lateral thinking) and asking why she does that. Could it have a direct effect?

In asking her not to place her right foot back, pain magically disappeared!

How about that! This had to be one of the more subtle postures that triggered significant pain we've ever seen. An easy fix, just lots of lookie loos, AKA observations.

**Overall Success! Our technician continued her career without nagging back pain.**

# You Don't Have to be a Credentialed Ergonomist to do Serious Ergonomics

I ran into a guy who was anything but an Ergonomist. We had a project together - I needed a custom seat insert for a bus driver and he an expert upholsterer (reported to be one of the best). He specializes in motorcycle seats and bikers come from around the country to have him develop special seats for them. There's also a nice apartment on the top floor of his shop which the customers can stay overnight if travel distance is long and the project is complex.

We had a great time together. When I observed him in his craft, I saw how he fit riders to their bikes and made custom seats.

A biker and hot rodder himself, a real gear head, he knew the ins and outs of a motorcycle seat and how a rider should be supported from the inner legs up through the back and down to the pedal controls. He knew his stuff. He emphatically stated he was not an Ergonomist; rather an upholsterer, who simply did Ergonomics (for bikers).

I must say I was impressed watching him go through his paces in fitting individuals to their bike seats. He would carefully prop the customers up on their bikes and carefully look at such things like body contact, back & leg support and weight distribution. After all, bikers are male, female, big, small, tall, short, height / weight / proportional

(HWP) and not so HWP, bow-legged, straight-legged, *all different shapes and sizes.*

Without formal schooling, just vast experience in both riding and fixing, he took his craft very seriously and hence his conviction and vast reputation in the biker world.

He studied his customers (anatomy), knew the nuances of how to use his hardware and simply melded the two into a custom seat. He understood the interaction between derriere, legs and backs to riding. Clearance and motion intricacies were known to him and I think he could fit a motorcycle seat to anyone, no matter what shape they or their derriere were in.

He professed to understand application of Ergonomics to seats for customers. In first hearing this over the phone when I first interviewed him for the project, I was a little skeptical. A lot of people have told me over the years they "Do Ergonomics." However I grew to respect his viewpoint and yes, even his knowledge and application skills.

***All this proves one doesn't necessarily need to be formally trained to do good Ergonomics-It just means that some people are doing some Ergonomics in their work without even realizing it.***

*But for complex problems and when someone has been injured, you do need a trained Ergonomist (just like a Mom or Dad can put a band aid on a cut, but they can't diagnose whether a sore throat is strep or meningitis - that requires a professional.*

For another story proving this point, see Ugly Real World Lack of Ergonomics in Chapter III.

Is our upholsterer an Ergonomist? Maybe yes. Maybe no. It's hard to say. He certainly was for his customers. And I do know this; he is intimate with his product and the interaction of his product with customers (the human body).

And to do really good Ergonomics you have to have this trait and he does, albeit limited to the motorcycle seat realm and limited applicable postures.

The important lesson here is that he's very intimate with his product. He's also intimate, by experience and observation about the human interface with his product. He fully understands by years of doing this to confidently apply Ergonomic principles to any seating device. To be this good you have to have this kind of intimacy.

To become intimate with any job or task, you have to actually experience it; you have to perform it. You have to get a real feel for what the end user or worker is going through. You have to understand that. To be good and to impact someone's life, you can't just look for a few minutes and make some sort of off-the-cuff recommendation of Ergonomic this or Ergonomic that. You can't or shouldn't "wing it" (like I've often seen).

There are only two ways that I know of to really, really understand the issue. One is through vast trial and error, also called experience. The other way is by a full analysis of what is going on, which may be simple or complex and definitely hands-on. Either way, project familiarity and intimacy is necessary before you have license to even think about fixing it.

During the project, I witnessed the application of real Ergonomics by someone who professed NOT to be an Ergonomist, but by someone who does Ergonomics in the motorcycle upholstery arena by project familiarity and intimacy.

You know, he's right and he has my utmost respect.

## Being a Detective

Our detective once said "You really have to know your stuff." "You need a knowledge base to relate it to." It's similar to troubleshooting your computer when you get the blue screen of death or a repeated error message. You have to delve into a history, a toolbox of knowledge and of course valid training (by hard knocks or some formal education).

These are also significant tools for a real Ergonomist and unfortunately generally not used by those of a wanna-be or forced-to-be nature. Additionally with all these tools and insight real

Ergos have a big, a really, really big advantage over folks like our computer technician, described here.

One day, I was talking with the techie who services our network, printers and of course viruses plus malware. He had just finished a brutal 2 year course in newly released specialized software from one of the big companies.

He told me it was worse than grad school. Endless evening studies, weekend classes. Time away from family, especially his little kids and of course his sweetheart. He sweated bullets during the studies, because the subject was so intricate, detailed, and complex. Once completed he got a fancy certificate with gold stamp, his name in fancy calligraphy and expensive frame for hanging on his company's wall noting he's expert in this type of software and hardware. Lo and behold, within a few months of course completion the software company releases a new version making the old one obsolete.

Just think, 2 years out of his life for nothing - Wotta Shame!

Yes, my techie friend had just spent two back breaking years working on this goal and in a flash; the software company pulled the rug out from under him. He told me he was so depressed because all his effort, late nights and family time sacrifices were for naught. I really felt bad for him

He looked at me and said, you guys have it made since what we do never changes, and you know he's right. The human body / anatomical principles don't change much (excluding double jointed acrobats). From the neck down, human anatomy has been very similar for a long time. No company is going to tell us we are obsolete. That is until (if you believe it) that we become cyborgs like The Terminator. It seems our profession *should* be around for a long time. *However, we really ought to pay more attention and do a better job of nurturing it.*

In working like detectives, we have to uncover the clues that negatively impact the human body. We have to become, maybe not an expert, but surely very knowledgeable about anatomy, its motions, its limitations, and the musculoskeletal & nervous systems that make it work.

My detective told me that if anyone becomes expert on this phase, especially the observations, they should be able to tackle any type of injury they find.

He said, "You got to have a good knowledge base, understand the problem and make sense of the data before you go and do a solution". Sage advice from someone who really understands how to get to the root cause of events, don't you think.

So, I implore all you professionals, especially the wannabes and forcedtobes to **_UP_** your game to the next level of knowledge and learn how to observe and analyze. You and your charges (injured workers) will be much better off if you do. Your professional expertise will take a big step forward and your spirit will also give a great feeling of accomplishment and contribution. You'll be doing something meaningful of many different planes.

## *Best of luck!*

Solve some things and this will be you one day

## Chapter VI

# 3 Real Life Case Stories, 3 Real Life  Successes

***Pain enough to threaten jobs and careers.*** Here are two actual projects, with two people in enough pain diminishing their ability to perform professional job tasks.

The first, Ellie B., works for a large municipality. An environmental engineer, she analyzes and documents scientific stuff, emphatically stating she "Loves Her Job" in no uncertain terms (I'm happy for her).  It also means she has high motivation to take care of herself.

The second is a close friend, of high intellect, a PhD from Stanford and Post Doc from Harvard. Unfortunately when you get too smart and too accomplished, you get to do things like spend an awful lot of time documenting your work in scientific journals and writing really long grant applications on a keyboard.

Both had really, really bad pain.  Pain enough for both to reach out to me.  One a complete stranger simply trying to alleviate her arm pain, the other I've known all my life, reaching out, being my friend, both needing help lessening their pain to continue with their careers.

Both are extensive keyboard jockeys, both in dire need of help. Both tried different things on their own but understandably unsuccessful. Both knew Ergonomics was some sort of answer, both reaching out to find that answer.

Here are their stories, and hopefully you can use them, gleaning inspiration, instruction or mentoring on how to approach what appears simple but in actuality a complex, yet very subtle Office Ergonomics project. It is my sincerest hope these types of pain scenarios become less frequent and have light at the end of the tunnel.

**The Case of Ellie B.**

You'll see how this really sad Ergo project began. Symptomology started out being an innocuous irritation progressing to years of full blown pain and debilitation. There won't be much humor in this story, but perhaps it will inspire some to really want and take necessary steps (not overstating their bounds or to find appropriate resources) to help someone, perhaps someone they know or love.

This Office Ergonomics project was done by remote control, in a different geographical state, clear across the country. It should speak to you that Ergonomics can be done this way effectively provided the practitioner's knowledge base is deep and people skills are sharp.

For Severe Industrial Ergonomics, see chapter VIII, Big Bad Machinery, which incidentally can also be performed remote control.

This serious and real story began with an inquiring email, finding our website through research and desperation. Included are actual emails exchanged and commentary on how her pain solutions were accomplished.

Activity occurred over several months with her main set back coming with helping her husband by using a pistol type air gun to clean stuff off, which she admitted: "She knew she shouldn't be doing this in the first place and that it would be bad for her wrists." 'Nuff said for self awareness. At least she knew at the time it was wrong. Unfortunately, like those and my Dad in the previous chapter Psychosocial Ergonomics, she decided to "Tuff it Out" compounding her pain.

Following is what Ellie B. wrote, along with the sequence of events. I leave it to you, dear reader to surmise the discomfort and trouble she was in.

Here's the first email coming from out of the blue:
**Email #1 from Ellie** B. **- June**

> *Ellie B. sent a message using the contact form at*
> *www.ergoinc.com*
>
> *I have been battling my employer (or really their lack*
> *of much assistance) for almost the last year regarding*
> *a problem I have had with mostly my right wrist (but*
> *also my left wrist and both arms at times). I have a*
> *work comp lawsuit just about at settlement - but there*
> *is one serious problem:*
>
> *I have not been able to get the problem corrected! I*
> *have had numerous doctor and PT visits. My*
> *employer finally got me an ergonomic assessment*
> *from an outside company, but the assessor, an*
> *occupational therapist basically told me I looked fine.*
> *I requested an ergo keyboard, which did help*
> *substantially with some of the problems. But I still*
> *have chronic, immediate pain from using my mouse.*
> *I don't know what to do and I can't find anyone who*
> *truly knows what they're doing as far as setting up a*
> *desk/mouse so I do not have perpetual pain. Do you*
> *know of anyone you can recommend that is in (My*
> *State)? Any help would be very appreciated.*
>
> *Thanks*

Like all emails, asking for advice or help, I return
called Ellie B. talking at length with her. She
appreciated our concern, but could not afford much
payment. She told me in detail about an assessment
by an Occupational Therapist who only took 15
minutes, didn't do anything and cost the company
$700. (WOW!)  $700 for doing nothing and for only
15 minutes?  I told her irrespective of payment I felt
I could help her, having performed lots of complex

projects by remote control (learning how the hard way, believe me) and was confident I could make her feel better. There really is a secret methodology to do this.

The big question is: why couldn't the Occupational Therapist who performed the original analysis really do something or is he a real charlatan? An obvious answer. Not only did he not do anything, he didn't even give a rip, and for that he cannot be forgiven. A true snake oiler or voodooist (see Chapter III – Snake Oilers). The result: *Ellie B. was essentially abandoned, left in pain*...and why was management so resistant to providing her some real help. Did they not care about her? I believe it was not intentional, but merely just wanting the situation to go away or just didn't have the time or inclination to deal with it (seen many times in the past). Sorta like sticking their heads in the sand and ignoring the circumstances. Remember, you can't see pain.

### *Another Wotta Shame!*
After some noodling, I queried her by email. She replied, offering some history

## Email #2 from Ellie - July

*After starting to develop a nearly constant discomfort in my right wrist, I did minimal internet research and found the vertical mouse. I asked my boss for this and received it in early summer 2013. This was the set up I had last fall, through the period when I was receiving PT, and perhaps or perhaps not coincidentally, through the time that I was in the most overall pain throughout this ordeal.*

*Through the months of PT, nothing was changing; in fact, I sometimes felt more/different pain than I had felt before. Not getting any better and getting frustrated by the constant pain I was working through, I requested and received the natural key board. Within just a few weeks of receiving this keyboard, most of the pain I had experienced in my left wrist/arm/elbow was gone and there were modest improvements in my right, particularly, the burning in my elbow mostly went away. I think this keyboard allowed my wrists to be in a straight line with my arms instead of kinked. Also, I think the center tenting of the keyboard, wrist rest, and downward slope toward the back of the keyboard helped things. The only thing that I didn't like about this keyboard is how large it was on the right and that I felt like my arm reaches out really far to reach the mouse.*

Another round of communication and then this from Ellie B.

## Email #3 from Ellie B. - Aug

*Hi Ian*

*Thanks for checking. I have gotten disgustingly little movement from my employer or from the pending lawsuit. My lawyer put in a settlement several weeks ago and I haven't heard anything yet. I asked in the settlement to have a trained, certified professional ergonomic specialist. I also tried following up with the OT that did the previous ergonomic assessment, but he just told me he was only contracted to do a one-time assessment and that was it (and I wonder what the heck the assessment was even for, then).*

*I just continue trial-and-erroring (on my own) to figure out an arrangement that doesn't hurt. After talking with you, I got rid of my vertical mouse and tried the standard mouse. That actually gave me more pain. Now I am re-trying a chair with arm support, trying to rest my arm on that and hang my hand off the edge and use my touch pad which is laying on my desk.... no big difference so far with anything.*

After a couple of follow-up phone calls, it became obvious real help was needed and most important she seemed "at the end of her rope" and would follow directions to help herself. A highly motivated individual, unlike many I've run into who just take a passive stance and don't really want to be bothered (Psychosocial Ergonomics); Ellie B. wanted to get things done.

At this point, I couldn't abandon her. I couldn't just stand idly by while someone is in pain. I offered to help her as best I could for the munificent price of a Starbucks Card. She agreed. Besides, if I didn't help her, who would? Probably no one is the answer.

She agreed to follow exact instructions. I requested she have a pal photograph close up of her hands, workstation, back, shoulder and a bunch of other things. She also sent a smiling frontal face shot. She's bright, attractive with a dynamite smile. I sent her specific charts and body maps with instructions on reporting, analysis and a bunch of other data gathering stuff.

I got back 30 pages of data and photos. She did her homework.

I next called her and we spent a couple hours on the phone going over her issues with notes and data in front of me.

Following I did some noodling, formulated a work plan, assessing her ongoing pain and sent her a list of specific equipment to purchase, which she did, to the tune of about $350. She immediately installed it and is with guidance using it properly.

Lo and Behold, her symptomology went down, way down (see before and after photos).

She really started to see improvement after the soreness after the episode using her sweetheart's blow gun settled down and we could get some real data on her workstation induced symptomology.

Here's her latest email.

### Email #4 from Ellie B.- Sept

*Ian: Following up quickly -*

> **The changes that were made at your recommendation have allowed me to partake in my normal life again.** *For the last several months, I couldn't enjoy my hobbies such as gardening or bicycling; I was in too much pain and fearful I would further aggravate my painful condition. While the pain isn't completely gone from my right wrist, it's substantially diminished. I am in relatively minor pain in my right wrist only when I am using my keyboard heavily at work, and the pain is almost completely gone from my arm and elbow. Even when I am keyboarding heavily enough to elicit pain, I can manage to work through the pain, and more importantly, I can enjoy myself outside of work. Thanks for helping me and I look forward to continuing to work with you so we can hopefully trouble shoot and take care of the rest of the right wrist pain.*
>
> *Thanks again!!*

What a wonderfully encouraging email to get, don't you agree?

It's really fun and satisfying to work a project like this and to give someone their life back.

A Starbucks gift card arrived in the mail with a warm hand written note on a Hallmark greeting card. It made me smile, not so much for the Starbucks card (although a nice gift) but more in knowing this really meant Ellie B. is getting better.

Here are some highlights and reasoning of what some simple equipment application did for her do along with some of her project specifics.

### *Medical Conditions / Symptomology (Ellie B.)*

*Left Arm*
- Mild to moderate pain in last 6 months

*Right arm*
- Moderate to significant pain & burning on medial and lateral elbow epicondyles (tennis elbow & golfers elbow)
- Burning pain though the dorsal and ventral (top & bottom) forearms
- Constant pain, soreness fatigue throughout entire wrist structure

### *Previous Mods Trialed / Results (Ellie B.)*
- Microsoft Natural keyboard installed with reduction in left and right arm symptomology
- Evoluent vertical mouse installed increasing pain prompting return to standard mouse

## *New Modifications Installed Per Our Instructions / Results (Ellie B.)*

- Kinesis Freestyle split keyboard- reduction in right and left arm pain
- Kensington Trackball Pro on right side - further reducing right wrist symptomology
- Kensington Trackball Pro moved to left hand further reducing right wrist symptomology with new mild triggering on left side – perhaps she is just susceptible to symptomology from these specific postures
- Super secret input device for other mouse functions - further reducing wrist symptomology

1. B4 - Evoluent Mouse

2. B4 - Original keyboard

3. B4 - Reverting back to original mouse

4. B4 - Microsoft Natural keyboard with Evoluent mouse

5. New - Kinesis Freestyle KB and Kensington Trackball

6. New - Getting used to the Kensington Trackball

## The Case of My Pal Tommy Joe

Tommy Joe's symptomology was equally serious when compared as Ellie B.'s. Steadily increasing, becoming more and more troublesome in his professional day, impacting his ability to keyboard. He (like many computer jockeys) became concerned if this was the beginning of the end. He seriously worried whether the diminishing keyboarding capability would impact his career. He is a prominent person in a prominent field very dependent upon his ability to keyboard.

We live in different states. No lengthy emails to me, just an initial quiet conversation at a social gathering, like most close friends would have. He quietly expressed his concerns. I quietly responded with a quick analysis and queried him about his workstation.

The photos are of the old workstation and new modifications

The modifications were installed and his symptomology initially went way down. However, he being my friend also has its nagging aspects. Every time I saw him, I had to ask about his symptomology (that's what friends do). After several months, he told me it settled down but didn't quite go away. I kept thinking about him and took him another modification for his workstation. It was a Contour Roller Mouse. We sat at the dinner table and opened the box and I took him through the

Roller's paces. The one observation he so astutely made was that it makes SO MUCH sense to bring every thing to the middle. It completely eliminates the outward arm rotation, a major contributor to right arm symptomology.

Old workstation triggering elbow (lateral epicondyle) & forearm pain

Previous touchpad forcing static loading on fingers, flexors and extensor forearm musculature

Really bad ulnar deviation (hand turned outward from the midline of the forearm)

Less inward rotation & ulnar deviation with a split keyboard having less stress on the forearm and elbow structures

Using the thumb to roll mouse leaving hands in home row position reducing loading on forearms

Right hand rolling with thumb - Kensington trackball still used on desktop for change of pace.

At last report, Tommy Joe continues using the Roller Mouse and is incrementally improving.

But like Ellie. B., he had a minor setback. It seems his energetic high school age son challenged him to a push-up contest. Well, Dad took up the challenge (what Dad wouldn't?). His right elbow let him know he shouldn't have. Like Ellie B. a recreational injury exacerbated the occupational injury.

So what?  They're both injuries, and if care is not taken regarding the occupational injury, personal or recreational activities can make the occupational injury (both being the same) worse.  The overriding thought for both Tommy Joe and Ellie B. here is: an injury is an injury is an injury and you have to let it heal, not subject it to additional strain when away from the workstation.

> *Unlike Vegas, if it happened at work,*
> *doesn't mean it stays at work.*

Ellie B. probably knew better, she admits it. Tommy Joe however succumbed to son's social pressure and probably should have known better, smart as he is.  In case you are interested, Dad out pushed up son two to one.

Here are some highlights and reasoning of what some simple equipment application did for Tommy Joe along with some of his project specifics.

### *Medical Conditions / Symptomology (Tommy Joe)*
- Moderate to significant pain at the outside right elbow (lateral epicondyle)
- Moderate to significant pain on the dorsal (top) of right forearm

### *Previous Mods Trialed / Results (Tommy Joe)*
- Installation of keyboard with built in touchpad device on keyboard right side without capability for position change - did not address symptomology

## New Modifications Installed Per Our Instructions / Results *(Tommy Joe)*

- Kinesis Freestyle split keyboard- right arm pain reduction
- Kensington Trackball on right side - further reducing right arm symptomology
- Contour Roller Mouse installed - further reducing right arm lateral epicondyle pain completely eliminating need to outward rotate right arm to reach Kensington Trackball
- Kensington Trackball moved to left side, completely removing all outward right hand rotation allowing right elbow to recover and to keep habitual usage of a known input device (Kensington)

---

## REASONS EQUIPMENT FAILED (For Ellie B.)

*Ellie B.'s Evoluent Mouse*

I've not had much luck with the Evoluent mouse. In concept it sounds and looks great. It gets the hand orientated in a vertical position, just like you would naturally shake hands with someone. We've had them in our offices and lab. We've all tried them out, but have not found significant application in the biomechanical realm. No great revelation, not sure if the design behind it is valid, don't know if it is effective. The concept, by rights should work. We simply have to wait for the right conditions for it to strut its stuff.

Consequently, we have run into folks who swear by them, and that's just *wonderful*!  Said before, you can't argue with success, and if you like the Evoluent and you perceive benefit from using it, then by all means keep using it and ***don't let any hotshot Ergonomist tell you otherwise***.  <u>If it works for you then this is indeed Ergonomics at its finest.</u>

I think the Evoluent is something everyone should at least try.  You don't know if it'll work if you don't.  Just don't keep it around if it doesn't.  Like Ellie B. or any good Ergonomist, keep trying other things until you (like Sherlock Holmes) come to a final conclusion based on objective thinking and analysis.  The Evoluent was seriously trialed and simply determined not to do what she wanted.  Nothing wrong with that, it's like a size 8 foot and a size 6 Nike shoe.  Both are perfect, but it is just not a fit.  This appears to be the case whenever I've run into the Evoluent.  It simply had to be replaced with something specifically to address the biomechanicals at issue.

*Ellie B.'s Microsoft Natural Keyboard.*

Ellie B. said the upright tented shape was somewhat beneficial.  In fact the shape has been beneficial for millions of keyboarders and is a nice little design.  However, like the scenario with the Evoluent, the

Natural just didn't quite do everything that I needed to specifically address Ellie B.'s biomechanicals. I have seen some people swear by them, but like the Evoluent, it just didn't do everything I needed a keyboard to do for Ellie B. Nike shoe size and foot size type of thing.

*Ellie B.'s Standard Mouse*

The standard mouse has been around for what seems forever and is still used by millions of keyboarders without incident. But like any other input device, if the user is prone to developing or already has symptomology the standard mouse can sometimes be a deal-breaker for career continuation or advancement.

There a couple of problems with standard mouse usage.

The first problem is not the fault of the mouse itself, but rather where it is located, usually on the desktop, forcing extended reach affecting shoulders, elbows and mostly forearms musculature. The result? A lot of pain in these areas, especially at the "tennis elbow" (lateral epicondyle) site.

Another problem is the way a lot of folks simply hold the mouse. Some think it is really a live mouse and they squeeze the beejeebers out of it using a death grip. Nothing wrong with holding onto something of value like this, however, really squeezing the mouse results in constant static loading on the hand / wrist / forearm structures which fatigue over time with resultant pain. The mouse doesn't mind, but your hand / wrist / arm surely will.

A third problem is the last one I'm going to describe, although there are a bunch more, is the actual use or movement of the mouse. Using the death grip many folks just move the mouse by anchoring the forearm on the desktop or chair arm, pivoting the hand at the wrist moving the mouse side to side, left to right in an arc. This is called in ergo circles, ulnar and radial deviation (deviation from the midline of the arm either in the direction of the ulnar and radius arm bones / left or right).

This pivot point wrist motion is obviously a detriment to the carpal tunnel when it repeatedly stretches and bends anatomical structures (like tendons and the median nerve) through the carpal tunnel. Too much of this left and right movement and Whammo! - You've got carpal tunnel syndrome (CTS).

The mouse front to back motion is generally performed with forearm locked on the desktop / arm rest with repeated finger flexion and extension. You can easily imagine, this affects forearm musculature, and associated tendons passing through the carpal tunnel with apparent problems after too much mouse handling.

Standard mouse usage in these movements described causes a vast majority of computer user hand / wrist / forearm problems we see.

## REASONS EQUIPMENT FAILED
### (For Tommy Joe)

*Tommy Joe's Touch Pad.*

I've never been a real fan of touch pads. Yes, I've used them from time to time for injured worker's workstation under certain circumstances. But overall and in general, I find they offer more problems than solutions for the average keyboarder. Touchpads work great for those who have severe arm movement issues, and if located in the middle or near the centerline of the keyboard, minimizing a certain type of reach, function wonderfully. Other successes with them include larger graphic type pads which a user can employ a pen type stylus for input and cursor movement; however this application is reserved for those with special hand / arm problems.

For the average keyboardist who has either developed or is predisposed to some sort of tendinitis or some such, the typical touchpad may be a triggering mechanism. Unfortunately the touch pad is omnipresent on 99% of all laptops, located in the middle just below the spacebar.

Laptop input devices making the most sense was a mini trackball located in the middle of the keyboard area just below the space bar, available for use by both hands. Other track ball laptop models had a small trackball located on the lower right hand corner. Some were glossy smooth and when combined with body oils or sweat, were difficult to control. A simple answer was to simply sand down the slick surface to a matte finish offering more friction between fingers and ball.

The touchpads seen in Tommy Joe's workstation force a completely static loaded finger to press down and move on the touch surface for cursor movement. This static loading (affecting hand and wrist structures) is the primary reason touch pads are not generally well liked by a significant number of power laptop users. Don't believe me? Ask a veteran power laptop user their opinion.

## REASONS WHY THIS EQUIPMENT WORKS
### (For Both Ellie B. & Tommy Joe)

*Trackballs*

Generally, I love most track balls, but only in specific circumstances and for specific reasons. I have installed and on the flip side also removed plenty over the years. Why removed, you ask? Simply because they were the wrong type of trackball for that specific individual and their specific biomechanical issues. Remember *"application is the only thing"*.

How can a trackball be wrong for someone you ask? Well, I'm glad you asked.

There are a myriad of different kinds of trackball input devices. Some have balls on the top, some have balls on the side, and some have balls on the front. Some balls are big, some are small, and some are medium size. Trackball design has advanced over the years and like many things Ergonomic, the ideal trackball of all available, is (get this) the one that works best for you. Finding it is the challenge.

So how do you find that out? Analysis and determination if the muscular action / pain can be successfully addressed by a trackball of specific configuration. Don't just blindly throw one into the fray and hope it works. That's not the way to do it!

The right trackball must be fit to the way the individual works (work tasks), hand action and analysis on specific symptomology details on what to offload. This is what was done in both these projects and final recommendations were one of my favorites, the Kensington Expert Mouse

Kensington Expert Mouse Trackball

Kensington Slimblade Trackball

The Kensington eliminates a lot of problems identified with the standard mouse and enables the hand / wrist arm aggregate to a more body neutral posture. Plus its programming of the 4 buttons is a plus. It eliminates the extreme and perilous hand postures, including ulnar and radial deviation postures (hitting the <esc>, <tab>, <backspace>, <enter>). It also eliminates the combination function <alt-6> keys, further saving adverse hand and wrist motions. All benefiting a worker in pain, allowing them to recover and importantly allowing physical and intellectual energy to be placed into keyboarding instead of addressing pain triggered by a bad mouse.

Interesting enough both of my "charges" here moved the Kensington trackball to the left side, trying a new approach in addressing right wrist / arm pain, something an ordinary mouse wouldn't let you do. Both really like that kind of flexibility.

A good trackball when *applied under the right conditions* can do wonders reducing a lot of pain. The Kensington trackballs may NOT be right for everyone, and I understand and have proven that, but they sure worked well for Ellie B. and Tommy Joe.

*Split Keyboards*

There have been numerous attempts of keyboard design over the years, with many of them now defunct, due to a bad design, bad marketing or lack of public understanding or acceptance (sales). The Kinesis Freestyle meets many criteria for addressing a lot of forearm and elbow pain. Mainly it allows a keyboarder to move hands away from each other to a position acceptable to the user. A standard one piece keyboard cannot do that. This elimination of inward arm rotation simply to reach the home row can be the difference between pain and non-pain. If the hands / wrists / arm aggregates are in non pain then the activation of the musculature is below threshold and has a high potential to recover and most importantly allow the user to continue keyboarding. Probably one of the most important corollaries for Ellie B. and Tommy Joe.

## REASONS WHY THIS EQUIPMENT WORKS
### Especially For Tommy Joe

*Contour RollerMouse Red plus™,*

Tommy Joe loves it and Ellie B. is currently trialing a model to see if we can't eliminate that last bit of elbow pain.

The Contour RollerMouse Red plus™, like the Kinesis Contoured™ keyboard has large palm rests allowing the keyboarder to rest hands in keyboarding position on the big fleshy parts of the palm (proper names are: thenar eminence and hypothenar eminence) completely offloading any contact pressure from the underside of the wrist, including the dreaded carpal tunnel.

The Roller Mouse also places cursor controls in the middle just below the space bar, having handy, scroll, left & right clicks, copy and paste access by the generally strong thumb. I wouldn't put one of these under someone who has a blown carpometacarpal joint (thumb knuckle), but for someone like Tommy Joe who has static loading and right arm rotation problems it _is_ perfect.

The central location of the cursor controls also eliminates any outward rotation saving extraneous motions of the arms for mouse (or other input device) usage. Properly set-up (emphasis on the properly) it can actually place the entire arm in a fully relaxed or neutral positioning offloading all subtle inadvertent forearm and upper arm loading.

All this once the user becomes fluent with the new non-conventional cursor control. Often times users develop personal touches on how to use the roller bar in conjunction with the cursor copy and paste keys, Ergonomics at its most creative.

Understand the Roller Mouse is actually a semi-custom application. It could benefit almost everyone and definitely addresses specific symptomology

However, don't let anyone else sit at your workstation and use it though, they'll probably insult you or give you some friendly ribbing about your "new mouse".

Right hand finger rolling mouse control with left hand finger clicking action

Large palm rests eliminate ventral pressure on wrists and carpal tunnel area

Left hand thumb action for mouse control and right hand click / roller action

Also with using the Contour's special roller bar, there are creative ways one can move the cursor and click by using one hand on the roller bar and the other on the inner guide shaft (pressing the entire roller actually is a left click). This works for some since it takes some dexterity to keep the cursor where it's placed when using the thumb to roll. Oftentimes the cursor will move by inadvertent action of the thumb when clicking with the roller bar. Using the roller bar with the other fingers allows more control for placement clicking. An alternative is to use the non rolling hand to click by pushing down the entire support bar the roller, well, rolls on. One little understood characteristic of the Roller Mouse is the multitude of ways to effectively use it, unlike a standard mouse or even trackball. It allows a rally high degree of flexibility for the users having a multitude of symptomology. For the appropriate user and application, it gets two thumbs up - not during use of course.

As a general rule one of my little operations secrets is always installing the Roller Mouse without initially removing the trackball or mouse. Since the Contour takes some getting used to and acclimate, it has proven very effective in still allowing habitual mouse usage once in a while. Eventually the regular mouse or trackball are eliminated and folks often ask how to get a Contour for their home set-up. However long they split time between the RollerMouse and their old mouse / trackball, their hands are not in such adverse posture and begin to feel better, always a plus.

Oftentimes the trackball is kept in conjunction with the Roller Mouse for simple posture variance.

## Bottom Line

The best news is, both Ellie B. and Tommy Joe experienced pain reduction from off-the-shelf, easily available, albeit relatively unknown hardware applications.

The most important element of each case was proper biomechanical analysis and appropriate application of hardware to hand action observed. Mostly it was a willingness to follow logical advice trying something new, nothing like those in Chapter IV, whose attitude prevented trying anything, even if it meant pain reduction.

Suffice to say, I appreciate these two individuals mostly because of their willingness for open communication, working through their issues.

But in my heart-of-hearts, I am saddened there are not more Ergos trying to help in a remote control manner or even in an in-depth manner like this.

Think of all the pain and suffering we collectively could take away in addition to improving profitability.

### *Now wouldn't that be something?*

Heart Warming Isn't It?

*So…Read on my Young Padawan to see what **Nasty** things happen when you Don't Use Ergonomics.*

## The *Bad, Ugly, Sad, Nasty* Real World LACK of Ergonomics

Here's what happens when you don't use
Ergonomics, or don't bother looking for it.

Y'all just read about the Dark Scary Real World
Lack of Ergonomics and nuclear power plants in
Chapter I - Hollywood Ergonomics…

*Well, here is a scarier even uglier one
resulting from lack of Ergonomics.*

This is not an uncommon theme - a sad result from
someone losing their job, self esteem, pride,
income, and family, all because they couldn't
perform their job due to lack of Ergonomics.
Many variations of this theme exist. You probably
even know of a similar encounter. It is indeed sad
to think this horrific thing could have been
prevented with the expenditure of a few dollars.

The story begins with a young lady, whom I have
had the honor of being labeled her friend and
mentor (of things Ergonomic). Her name is Joy.
She began her career in the corporate ladder,
armed with a degree in health sciences, being
introduced to the science by a difficult matter.
After 15 years of practical experience and training,
she is now a SME (Subject Matter Expert), a
CBRES (Certified Behavioral Ergonomics
Specialist), among other things, taking care of a lot
of power keyboarders and mousers in a really big

company. At last report her analyses and solutions number in the thousands.

She had an older sister with a career of a high powered shipping coordinator, spending most of the day and probably lots of overtime on breakneck computer keyboarding. Sister developed severe bilateral Carpal Tunnel Syndrome. Intense unfathomable pain followed.

Like many who are riddled with severe pain, she tried to work through the burning and numbness, but the Carpal Tunnel Syndrome won the battle.

Naturally, doctors, PT, hand specialists and nerve specialists were consulted, followed by an action plan of bilateral carpal tunnel surgery with both wrists operated at the same time.

Well, guess what? Since carpal tunnel surgery has historically been a real low percentage hit, Sister unfortunately ended up on the short end with debilitating pain worse than before. She began to take pain medication - Hydrocodone - 2 years to be exact. Initially provided an unlimited prescription supply with the advice to take whenever needed.

"Don't worry about the drug" the doctors said. "It's completely safe." "Take as much as you want." This enlightened attitude existed in the 90's.

## Beginning of the End

Meanwhile Sister kept doing her job as best she could, with a noticeable drop in efficiency, accuracy and productivity. But the medicine was keeping her pain at least to a tolerable level, provided she took enough to really make a noticeable difference. Everyone does that - got a massive headache? Just pop a handful of Tylenol. That should knock your headache out fast. Unfortunately, continual doses of Hydrocodone can have devastating effects.

Sister was at least functioning. Then the drug became restricted and the doctors immediately cut her off without any optional treatment. Not much choice for Sister except over the counter meds, which didn't even dent the pain.

The combination of no pain relief and withdrawal proved too much.

Desperately, she next turned to alcohol to help alleviate the severe discomfort. Desperation indeed, since she previously had rarely taken a drink. 'Tastes terrible," she would say. "Why would anyone want to drink this stuff?" Definite desperation to find relief.

Like the pain meds, her thinking was, the more of this, the less of that (pain). A common downwards spiral for someone in pain without any alternative for relief. Sister's social and professional lives took big hits. The searing burning pain wouldn't let go. She could not function well at work, lost her job, and her income. Her dependence on alcohol turned into an addiction. Like many alcoholics, her marriage dissolved and eventually after repeated episodes of rehab and through battles of serious depression, she fell into a coma, and slowly slipped away, devastating her family and friends - and Joy lost someone very close, her only sister.

## Lack of Ergonomics Attributed as the Cause

This all occurred because lack of ergonomics essentially allowed Sister's wrist injuries to occur, triggering all the events leading up to her final exit. Such an unfortunate occurrence, to think at all her suffering and premature death could have been ***prevented*** by a good Ergonomically sound set-up with proper (emphasis on the proper) equipment installation at her computer workstation.

As Sister's life was obviously deteriorating before her eyes, my friend Joy became distraught and upset at the circumstances allowing her sister's downward spiral. All the while my friend deeply wished there were something that she could have done to help her sister.

Fortunately, Joy found the opportunity to get involved with Ergonomics and she wanted to help prevent injuries like the ones that eventually killed her sister. Having seen CTS first hand and intimately, this concept stayed with her in the back of her mind.

Out of the blue, one day in a corporate environmental safety and health meeting, the subject of Ergonomics was brought up and the meeting Chairman asked if anyone was interested in heading up this program. Joy still had an inner reaching desire to help her sister (but couldn't). If she couldn't help Sister, maybe then she could really help someone else from having the same problems. She immediately volunteered.

With bold moves, she embarked upon an adventure and journey, getting training learning the science going to conferences, making appropriate workstation modifications, "spreading the word" and helping fellow workers stave off debilitating injuries like Sister developed. Usually with minimal budget (Ergonomics budget is hard to come by) she would use her left brain with creative activities to at least bring awareness to the masses. Once she made a clever video called "Ergo Nightmare" to bring out Ergonomics in an enjoyable, cheesy, corny and comical manner. Quite successful, she starred as the "Ergo Fairy" and presented "Ergo Nightmare" at several major professional conferences to rave reviews. She has since put some alphabet soup after her name getting some real training and continues to this day managing the administration and coordination of

Ergonomics Services and a staff, doing Real Ergonomics.

I am naturally quite proud of her, but better than that, Sister, before passing away spoke of being very proud Joy was doing this so others wouldn't have to go through the same pain, trauma and life altering circumstances. A touching moment, making my friend Joy realize that her passion and "carrying the banner" is a legacy to Sister.

Now, I would truly consider my Friend a success story. Unfortunately it took a devastating event to bring this about.

All we can do (besides doing really good Ergonomics) is to remember how proud Sister was of my Friend in going the extra mile to help others.

Godspeed Sister.

## Chapter VII

# Big Bad Machinery &
# Little Bad Machinery

Big bad machinery

Big bad machinery

Little bad machinery

Little bad machinery

Much of the pain we feel is largely caused by machines we use, big ones and little ones.

Obviously Ergonomics affects all aspects of the working world.

Most folks have associated the word Ergonomics in familiar office workstations even if unsure of meaning, benefits or how use it to their advantage. Other areas include almost every industrial type of activity like big machine shops, assembly lines (computers, toys, cars, trucks boats, trains, planes,) warehouses, lumber yards, hospital operating rooms, restaurants, food handling, and manufacturing, along with virtually anything else in the world. Pretty much anywhere or any time someone is doing something (performing a task), is affected by Ergonomics, good and bad.

Here are some suggestions from our project portfolio offering some ideas or inspiration for methodology developing solving complex Ergonomics projects. Big Bad Machinery of course relates to the vast industrial world where, well, big bad machinery exists. This big bad machinery oftentimes overwhelms workers anatomy to the point of breakdown, easily seen by makin', pushin', shovin', carryin' or manipulatin' big and usually heavy things.

Little Bad Machinery relates to the small hand tools, actions and tasks found at almost every computer workstation, also contributing to overwhelming anatomy causing excruciating sometimes debilitating pain.

In retrospect, these projects were really fun; I'm amazed and pleased at the outcome. Yet I wonder why solutions like these are uncommon, being few and far between. Maybe it's because all explorations of different avenues are not taken. Explorations and different approaches are also time consuming, especially if nothing like these things have ever been done before. Maybe people give up too soon before a real solution is explored for development.

As Calvin Coolidge once said:

*"Nothing in this world can take the place of persistence. Talent will not: nothing is more common than unsuccessful men with talent. Genius will not; unrewarded genius is almost a proverb. Education will not: the world is full of educated derelicts.*
**Persistence and determination alone are omnipotent".**

*Exploration is key, don't give up!*

You just have to keep trying. Although you might need to find some friendly help, maybe in the way of an engineer or perhaps someone with an engineering background or possibly just a tool junkie (handyman) to help with some ideas. Maybe a designer with a new approach.

Mostly it helps to have an objective set of eyes to shed some light or have a different approach on how to modify some of the big bad or little bad machinery causing the problem.

Therefore the best advice I can give to a fledgling Ergo is to be persistent, explore all avenues and then determine the best course of action by assembling your resources (oftentimes a good methods engineer or maybe a trusted vendor / manufacturer of equipment). Then you can build a mock-up or a prototype and try it out, and when it doesn't work (highly likely it won't the first time) keep trying.

Ancient Chinese Philosophy dictates

> *"Young Grasshopper, understand,*
> *it is just as important to know*
> *what **NOT** to do as it is to know*
> *what **TO** do.*
> *Perhaps more important"*

There will always be a solution, not just a solution, but a GOOD solution, provided you keep trying, following-up and exhausting all possible alternatives.

# *Press On!!*

## Here are a couple of case solutions with: *Big Bad Machinery.*

**Big Shearing Machines** have hand grip activation (also labeled mushroom switches) cause carpal tunnel syndrome with the two handed impact to trigger a large cutting shear or stamp, – swap out with photo cells. Sometimes a holder is required, just design one and stick it in. No hand impact involved.

**Bike Cops** are often afflicted with hand, wrist and forearm pain. Retrofit their handlebars with special shock absorbing padding. Put shocks on the front forks. Put shocks on the rear tire frame. Issue vibration damping gloves. The overall approach is to lessen the repeated road shocks transmitted up through the wrists and shoulder structures.

**Bulldozer Operators** with back injuries cannot sit in the big machine. Work with a seating specialist and develop a custom vibration and shock isolating seat to install in his big bad machine - a seat that supports and fits the specific needs of the driver. It may need heat in the winter time and cooling in the summer. It may also need custom cutouts for arm clearance so they can work the front ender controls.

**Motorcycle Cops** are always dumping their bikes or getting hit by errant drivers. Injured backs ensue. A custom motorcycle seat is the answer in working with a custom seat manufacturer. Sometimes these seats need a nifty back support.

**Truck Mechanics** tend to blow out knees from standing and slipping on greasy front suspensions. Here you need to make a custom platform for the mechanics to stand on for stable footing.

**Bakers** often have hand/arm/wrist/shoulder injuries from slicing hundreds of frozen cakes during graduation and special holidays. A custom slicer from the fish industry is just the ticket. Totally eliminates bending over and cutting big sheet cakes on a table

**Short Haul Truck Drivers** often injure their back and can't pull open stuck / rusty cargo container doors. Just make a leverage tool that slips into the existing slots of cargo containers giving them more leverage with less pull and a better place to grab.

**Cooks** after injuring their backs can't bend over to access the under counter fridge for special food prep ingredients. Use a small fridge on a rolling adjustable height hydraulic cart. No bending needed. Just roll out of the way during off shift.

**Mail Carriers** sometimes have to haul mail over rough terrain and strain backs pulling and pushing typical mail carts. Modify a baby runner with 3 big wheels to navigate swamps, puddles and rough gravel surfaces. Eliminates all excessive pushing and shoving and can be used by someone with a bad back.

**Veterinarians** develop severe hand maladies using a hypodermic syringe to draw fluids from exotic animals like Bengal tigers only using one hand considering the other hand is on the tiger jaw to keep the teeth away, one leg is on the front two of the tiger, the other leg is holding down the hind leg and the entire body is leaning against the tiger to keep the thrashing down. Try drawing with one hand accurately. Ever had a blood draw when the technician missed the vein? Tigers don't like it either. Simple solution. Design a special syringe that allows inject and draw with only one hand using the typical three finger squeeze posture everyone knows. Piece of cake.

**Machinists** have back and leg injuries from working on the bottom of big metal parts held up by crane. Only thing needed here is a mobile stand that moves the pieces up and down, round and round, allowing machinists to always work from the top. Rolling fixtures from station to station also saves time, manpower and really helps LEAN.

**Oil Rig Roughnecks** have arm and shoulder injuries from spinning up and down valve shafts, which are usually stuck or require a lot of effort. Easy answer: Weld a big steel nut into the shaft and provide a high quality cordless impact wrench, with two batteries since having only one obviously ensures it will never be charged at the right time.

**Construction Workers** injure back lifting 100# jack hammers off the truck and carry them to the cutting site. Just build a rolling cradle and lift mechanism that lifts and secures the jackhammer to the truck. No carrying needed.

**Dump Truck Drivers** fall off the sides of the bed while clearing the top rim of debris and inspecting level of load for DOT clearance. Provide a tool shaped like a golf club to rake the top rail of debris, also provide a large mirror on a big stick (inspection mirror) allowing them to see the load over a 8' high side rail. No climbing required.

**Package Handlers** develop repetitive strain injuries (RSI) from grasping and moving high volumes (thousands) of parcels per day. Design a conveyor system that allows minimal handling and appropriate staging for all packages. If the conveyor system is angled then the worker can self select the right height for them (after being trained to understand what that is, of course) - Minimizes handling and injuries.

**Mammography Technicians** have to stand all day setting up exams on big Mammograph machines and often need to contort themselves repeatedly for viewing angles developing back and leg pain. Look at the way they stand and advise on corrections.

**Assembly Line Workers** often develop backs working all day at too high or too low workbenches. Shim up the workstations or install adjustable height or maybe even custom bench top platforms for individual workers with dedicated workstations.

**Aircraft Assemblers** often injure themselves lifting and setting big heavy jig components. All that's needed is to design /develop a custom carrying mobile trunnion. No lifting required.

**Ultrasound Technicians** often afflicted with the "crucifix injury" - a Repetitive Motion Injury (RMI) from stretching the arms out to both sides with on hand manipulating the transducer on a patient and the other stretched out to the computer controls on the ultrasound machine control consol. Specialized postural training programs considering the subtle nuances of how each sonographer works in terms of placement, posture and manipulation can alleviate the problem.

## Here's How a Project (new tool development) Sometimes Goes Down

Take for example an oil filter wrench, heavy duty 1" pneumatic impact wrench or any other tool to work on Big Bad Machinery. Note the methodology here is virtually the same for all Big Bad Machinery along with Little Bad Machinery tool / task modification development.

Mechanics have been doing this for years, welding, bending re-shaping some of their favorite tools - sometimes they work - some times they fail miserably, but that's the whole point. During my time being a mechanic, miserable failures happened more often than not - the point is to pick your self up by the bootstraps and keep on making trials and efforts until you have absolutely run out of ideas… at which time you ask your fellow mechanics for advice. Sometimes your brethren will laugh and make fun of you. You know the type, so you just move on to find those who insightful and helpful. These are the ones you go back to and even buy them coffee for their input.

They say, "You should have tried this or that." They forget that you went through serious trial and error getting to this point and only see your current project stage. At any rate they beat you about the ears and tell you how to improve the device, which is what you wanted in the first place. Try another modification, and then if it doesn't work ask another fellow mechanic, hopefully one who will be a little gentler on their critique on your creative efforts. Chances are said mechanic will eventually help you develop a tool that works way better than any other on the market or that even exists.

## _In actuality, this is a classic design sequence_

All in the name of Ergonomics, simply to make the job easier with less strain on the body, more efficient, more productive and also highly important_, less frustrating._ After all, that's one of the reasons you started out with a new design activity wasn't it?

This scenario applies to any and all professions trying to implement or do Ergonomics, whether truck mechanics, carpenters, plumbers, factory workers, machine operators, or anyone in the trades using their hands to perform a task.

# And here are a couple of cases involving: *Little Bad Machinery* (LBM)

Insidious dangerous and injury producing tools are found in virtually all office workstations. These are quite common since the current state of tools for the office tasks exist simply because they are the cheapest way out. When looking for desktop tools at Office Max, the overriding parameter is of course cost. And with low cost comes either low quality or a design that surely has no thought for safety of the user. Virtually all of the cheap desktop tools adversely affect user anatomy over even a short term when used on a regular basis. Not only that, they seem to go out of their way to injure you.

We have seen hundreds of office workers with severe pains in their hands, wrists and arms from continued use of such Little Bad Machinery tools.

Here are two examples of workers pointing out their areas of significant pain, from the requirements of using such all day, repetitively.

Carpal Tunnel Syndrome from using LBM-staple remover held in hand

Lateral epicondylitis - lots of pain at the elbow and down through the top of the forearm

Presented here are Little Bad Machine examples I have seen cause a lot of pain in folks like the photos above, along with their easy solutions.

## Hole Puncher LBM

| | |
|---|---|
| The cheap type requiring a lot of force to press down often used in one handed squeeze or with elbow up causing overloading / injury to hand & wrist musculature | Electric model punches 12 sheets at a time (2 & 3 holes) with no effort - much easier and faster saving the hands and wrists ($75) |

## Staple Remover LBM

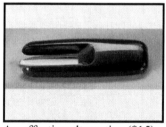

| | |
|---|---|
| Typical cheap staple remover forcing severe pinch grip and lots of repetitive usage - big contributor to carpal tunnel syndrome, tendinitis or tenosynovitis | An effective alternative ($15) staple remover by Rubbermaid, completely eliminates any type of grip, simply slides, removing the staple cleanly - the **BEST** remover on earth, bar none! |

## Hand Stapler & Electric Stapler LBM

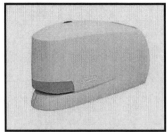

Typical cheapo standard issue hand stapler requiring extended reach and raised elbow in most cases directly and adversely affecting wrist, forearm and shoulder structures, especially with freestyle holding and power gripping (yes we have these in our offices too)

Electric stapler ($35) completely eliminates any adverse hand, wrist and arm action plus increases productivity since stapler handling is eliminated - yes we also have these in our offices, really making professional life a LOT easier

## Excessive Tight Grip Pens LBM

Death grip on ordinary pens contributes to CTS, tendinitis and other painful things - stressing everything in the hand, wrist & fingers

Foam covered pens totally eliminates severe pinch grip - custom diameter for different hand problems, hand size and grip strength - with special pens preventing too much downward force ($8)

## Sort all & Sorting Rack LBM

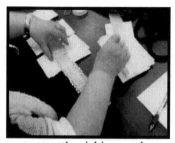

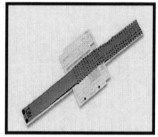

Constantly picking up the sorting dividers with left handed two finger pinch grip stresses on the forearm flexor musculature also contributing to carpal tunnel syndrome

Typical desktop sorter being used at left forces lifting each divider with a power pinch grip tearing up the forearm musculature also affecting and effecting carpal tunnel

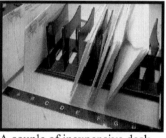

For a solution, just get a couple of these, line them up label the slots and just place the documents in - no pinch grip required, and less hassle getting them out - productivity improvements ($15)

A couple of inexpensive desk racks and a alphabet ruler provides an easy alphabetizing rack eliminating all the left hand pinch grip and CTS stressors it's much better and also way faster than using the device shown above!

## Rubber Banding LBM

Continually stretching rubber bands like this really blows out your forearm extensors and small hand musculature

Stretching and doubling up the rubber bands continues the damage to hands and wrists, especially for CTS – Using 1 hand to hold the papers, forces a difficult and injury prone single hand stretch

Simply use the right size rubber band for the job - it's not a one size fits all proposition - the right size requires less stretching and less problems for the hands, eliminating the doubling up ($3 per size package) - a lot cheaper than CTS medical bills

If you have to band, place the paper pile in the alphabetizing holder allowing 2 hands on the rubber band instead of 1 hand like the top photos

## <u>Pulling 3-Ring Binders from Shelves LBM</u>

Pulling heavy 3 ring binders off shelving requires power pinch grip, extended reach contributing to CTS, and arm / shoulder tendinitis

Catalog holders for the 3 ring material completely eliminates any extended reach to the shelf and the forces on the hand / wrist / arm aggregate, making information more easily accessible improving productivity ($40)

## Help Yourself

If you find yourself using these cheapo tools or performing these tasks with any kind of regularity, and you're in pain or at least developing some soreness or discomfort, do yourself a big favor (or for someone you love) spend a few bucks and get the tools to eliminate the problem. After all what is your pain worth? Once you try these things, you'll never go back. I know, I've seen them in action and we even use them ourselves, in taking our own medicine you might say.

If you do it, you'll really be glad you did. The effect and benefits are immediate, as in right NOW!!

# Chapter VIII

## Honoring William Safire
### (1929 - 2009)

Long ago being young, full of spit and vinegar while trying to learn the science of Ergonomics, I was reading everything available on Ergonomics which really wasn't much. Then the New York Times ran an article about Ergonomics by the late William Safire.

Mr. Safire was a recipient of the 1978 Pulitzer Prize, a presidential (Nixon) speechwriter and NY Times columnist of which his satirical viewpoints were read and enjoyed by many.

He wrote about Ergonomics in its (public awareness) infancy. The article appeared in the Nov. 21, 1982 issue of the NY Times in his "On Language" column. The accompanying illustration is original. The beginning of his article has been omitted since it doesn't deal with Ergonomics directly but infers meaning by describing elements of slang and the English Language.

Photo - Fred Conrad, New York Times

Over the years I have enjoyed his analytics, his wit, writings, and advice and I honor him. He is someone I would have also loved to have lunch with. I have tried to model my writings inspired by his style and wit.

Here is the 2nd half of the 1982 column by Mr. Safire that I have treasured for many years, verbatim. I hope it inspires you.

## That Icy Tingle - New York Times
### by William Safire - 21Nov82

## Nomiconomics

Country-music vocalists are not all Republicans. When Mac Davis performed his latest release, "The Beer Drinkin' Song," at the annual awards show of the Country Music Association, he drew a gasp from the 4,400 stompin' spectators when he sang that one of the things that would drive a man to drink was *Reaganomics.*

George Bush, campaigning for President in 1980 described candidate Reagan's supply-side theories as ***voodoo economics***;  two years later, Urban league president John Jacob was saying that *Reaganomics* "is giving voodoo a bad name."

The most rampant combing form used to be —*arama*, then it became —*oriented*, which gave way to —intensive. In the economic field, however, there is one combining form that sail on through Presidencies —nomics.

In the summer of 1969, I wrote a memorandum for my White House colleagues using the term *Nixonomics* to hail the ingenious replacement of the Democrats' "new economics." About that time columnist Evans and Novak were the first to use *Nixonomics* in Print. Walter Heller, a father of the "new economics," was quoted in Time magazine in November 1969, using *Nixonomics* disparagingly, Since that time, the term I used with such high hopes has fallen on hard times.

The key to phrasemaking was the *n* at the end of Nixon, which matched the *n* at the end of econ and produced a word easy to say. During the Ford years, the combining form lay dormant, though there was a half-hearted effort at *Fordonomics.* In Mr. Carter's time, *Carternomics* was occasionally used but it did not sing; *Jimmynomics* was also used to disparage the President's economic policy. Nothing really caught on after *Nixonomics* because the *n* was lacking at the end of the President's name.

Along came Reagan, Nobody can spot the coiner for *Reaganomics* because the coinage was a instantaneous as "As Maine goes, so goes Vermont." the rush of usage of *Reaganomics* seems to have overcome previous barriers and changed the way *economic*s is split: what used to be the econ—omics is now *economics*, and whatever work or name you like can be used in place of the *eco*,  Hence *Volckernomics, Trudeaunomics* even - shades of back - formation - *Hoovernomics.*

Personally, I resist the use of any —*nomics* coinage that has no *n* at the end of the first word.  Economist Henry Kaufman puts forward *Kaufmanonomics*, and economist Martin Feldstein may be credited with Feldsteinomics, but neither Mondalenomics nor Kennedynomics comes trippingly off the tongue. (Glennomics is a sure thing.)

Meanwhile another use of the combining form is coming upon us.  I was buying a stereo for my car, James Meyersberg of Auto Sound Systems in Bethesda Md., told me that in one high-priced model:

*"The ergonomics are beautiful."*
Pressed for an explanation, he said:

*"The pushbuttons feel nice."*

*Ergonomics* — based like "economics," on
the Greek word for "work" - is the
scientific study of man working in his
environment. The word has been with us
since 1950, and as the "interfacing"
between the faces of people and the face of
a machine increases, the work will become
more familiar. Right now ask anybody
what ergonomics is and the answer will be
***"The crackbrained economic schemes of***
***President Ergon."***

Actually and unfortunately, 30 years later, Mr.
Safire was accurate in his prediction and that some
folks really would think Ergonomics really is

***"The crackbrained economic schemes of President***
***Ergon."*** (See Chapter II - State of the Art).

Authors note:

I thank Mr. Safire for his insight and contributions.
I believe the world to be a lesser place without him.

## *Chapter IX*
## Beaucoup Bucks for Businesses

You may be bored or want to skip this section if you are an Ergo Pro or Injured Worker only concerned with workstation or work task stuff, being disinterested in the macro sense of Ergo applications, and who can blame you?

***BUT*** if you have a larger business view in mind, and maybe you want to do your share to keep the company and yourself healthy you're in the right place asking why the title of this chapter is Beaucoup Bucks for Businesses.

### So, How Can Business Really Cash In With this Science?

Well, I'm glad you asked that! I really am! After all company health is directly related to your physical and mental health (and vice versa) and your ability to get not only work, but effective, quality work done and done fast.

Image courtesy of Graphicstock.com

Typically viewed as difficult to measure, Ergonomics is generally not the first thing people reach for to increase profitability. The intent here is not to really go into detail on how to track benefits, but to show how the overall cash value of workstation modifications (AKA Ergonomics) can be seen and measured by operations professionals and the workers in pain.

*Let's start with the core issues*

As a general rule, most businesses have several problems:

They don't know how to
- Treat workers
- Keep them happy
- Keep them healthy
- Make them more productive
- Include them in solution development

Most of all, they are unfamiliar in how to make, not just save, but *make* beaucoup bucks in doing all the above.

American businesses tend to be very short sighted in this manner.

Three things are required for each and every worker to be really, really successful:
- Performance
- Productivity
- Attainment

Without getting into a business operations teaching mode, suffice it to say that to get all of these, workers with their jobs have to be:

- Happy
- Healthy
- Satisfied

With Biomechanical Ergonomics (neck down stuff - neck up stuff is another story), health is the real issue.  Health is a direct correlation to someone effectively performing a task (irrespective of productivity), normally called work or a job.  Another correlation is how "easy" (different from effective) it is for someone to perform that job, avoiding or addressing injury otherwise called simply keeping their health.

I know it's obvious, but here goes - if a worker is not healthy, then they cannot perform their job tasks effectively or with a high degree of efficiency.  Suffice it to say if workers (no matter what the profession – from assemblers to janitors to computer jockeys) cannot perform well, then widgets will not get built properly, floors won't be cleaned properly or stock analysis may go wrong.  Productivity takes a dip, quality is compromised and product not getting out the door costs a lot of money, generally called hidden costs.

Or they may be healthy, but the job itself is cumbersome and requires more effort than need be, sucking energy, time and productivity (hidden costs) out of our worker. Are you as productive as you should be? Maybe, maybe not.

Hidden costs can break the bank. Now there is the well known cost avoidance in preventing a bad case of Carpal Tunnel Syndrome, but think of what increased productivity could be if your entire workforce were hitting on all cylinders…it could really be measured in Beaucoup Bucks.

Here are some examples of hidden or indirect costs:

- *Loss of productivity when a person tries to work in pain*
- *Loss of productivity when co-workers do the work of an employee who is recovering from an injury*
- *Cost to hire a new employee when an injured employee cannot return to work (usually equivalent to 1 year salary)*
- *Increase workers' compensation cost if an injury results in an increase in the insurance experience modifier*
- *Difficulty hiring workers if the facility has a reputation in the community for injuries*
- *Cost of an incident investigation is 4 to 10 times workers' compensation cost (number of people involved in the incident investigation)*

Take for instance the real and direct impact on productivity, performance, throughput, delivery of services, and the bottom line. It can affect an entire business by enhancing the most important business component - the ability of workers to do their job, no matter what it is.

Ergonomics helps workers function better by humanizing their workstations and tools, stopping their pain and improving their ability for task performance. Applications can be had for both white and blue collar workstation environments. The use of Ergonomic principles reduces time loss (worker comp payments), lost time (uncaptured production time spend performing unproductive tasks), absenteeism and saves hard dollars which can be measured through standard management systems. These applications allow workers to perform better, improve productivity, maximize quality and maintain customer service, all real world business principles and thus measurable by real dollars.

Well then, how do you answer when asked "How do you measure the financial gains?"

Read on Pilgrim, *Please!*


## Measuring the Financial Gains

Business concepts being productivity, cost savings and performance can be easily measured and seen on auto, electronic or similar assembly lines. Or even on (dis) assembly lines including those in chicken processing factories. Enhancements from Ergonomics can be seen here within hours, even minutes and most importantly can be translated into dollars by even a rookie accountant. But how can you track cost savings and benefits in the white collar arena where only paper is shuffled and no real goods are manufactured, in places where information is transferred instead of actual three dimensional products? Here it appears more difficult to measure performance of someone sitting at a desk, talking on the phone and working at the computer all day.

With these concepts you are measuring ways in which the workers produce things, like briefs, reports or other paper deliverables. You can also measure the effectiveness of service to customers in bank tellers, legal assistants, secretaries or accountants.

A simple standard business methodology (one type out of many) of performance and productivity measurement is a documented daily, weekly, monthly management operating system. Such a system can track the hours of employees (regardless of task) in a white collar computer environment. Measurement of hours and what workers accomplish during those hours can be used to determine the influence of occupational injuries.

## Lost Time (productivity measurement), not Time Loss (time off work measurement).

Very simply, without broaching worker intellectual capability, management must determine specific and reasonable expectations of what can be accomplished during man-hour time units, considering work tasks, worker skills/capabilities, workload, and deadlines. This attainment is established and (earned) hours are measured against the goal as a percentage.

The result is a "lost time" concept. Like the worker compensation "time loss" in which a worker is absent from the workplace and productivity for that individual is zero, lost time is a measurement of how a worker is negatively impacted by an occupational injury or inability to easily and effectively work due to bad (stupid) Ergonomics.

Measurements before and after Ergonomic interventions can definitely showcase improvements in individual performance, measured against attainment or management goals. A measurement system like this can bring the benefits of Ergonomics from a purely subjective concept into one that can be measured by hard dollars, big hard dollars.

These concepts are well known and can be applied to the application of Ergonomics. Hundreds of books are available on measuring business activity.

It is not the intent to describe business measurement here, other than that it exists and is currently in use. Knowledge of good measurement techniques abounds in most business organizations and is taught in all business schools across the country.

*It the unusual application of these standard business tools to ergonomic principles that is significant and really something to see.*

## **Throughput and its Measuring is a Key**

Most organizations are interested in higher production- more, faster, with fewer people and with better quality.  Thus the basis for the whole field of industrial engineering.

Ergonomics can help this.  Real, not voodoo Ergonomists are expert in helping client companies do this.  Unfortunately, Ergonomics school or experience usually doesn't prepare us for determining profitability of business aspects.  Better to team with someone who is an expert in these manners, who has the training, education and experience in business measurement.  It's very difficult to do it all yourself.

In the real world of business, generally, someone just has to show us how they want to measure benefits and gains in their particular company.  The relationship of performance, productivity and attainment is only one of many methods

You also have to know how the client wants to measure what and by which unique indicator before installing a measurement methodology. You don't want to measure your work in English when they already measure their productivity in Swahili

## Bottom Line Benefits

Investments in Ergonomics can be ***returned three to tenfold, maybe more*** in improved performance, throughput and corollary savings, although this is just the tip of the iceberg. Ergonomics also prevents future occupational injuries and productivity problems. Cost avoidance is another way to measure Return on Investment (ROI).

Image courtesy of clker.com

Put them all together and Ergo solutions improve productivity, reduce lost time, time loss absenteeism, and presenteeism and save hard dollars

measurable through standard management systems. They can lead to lower workers' compensation premiums and reduced medical costs.
Understanding these concepts allows any Ergo type a better way and higher level on which to strut your stuff. Savings over even a short time period can reveal financial gain in six figures.

That kind of money is worth looking into, don't you think?

Image courtesy of Graphicstock.com

The point here is the value in tracking modifications, proving their benefits because most businesses are run with a big eye on the bottom line of financial statement.

If you can improve that, then you are indeed on your way to becoming an Ergo Pro who understands business needs and who is better armed to help injured workers. And isn't that what the *Bottom Line of Ergonomics* is supposed to be all about?

# But What About a Company wide Ergonomics Program?

A common problem in the workplace today is the employer's inability to identify, measure and correct the factors that impede worker performance and place them at risk of injury. This problem has a direct affect on the employer's bottom line.

Wouldn't a company wide program track improvements? Wouldn't it actually help us identify problems and then fix them for us? Isn't a program a be-all and end-all perhaps nirvana of all things Ergonomic?

Have you heard this before? These are questions uttered in many a safety or EHS meetings in many a company. Common queries triggered by knowing there is a need, but not really knowing what to do about it or possibly not really understanding (see State of the Art - Chapter III).

Ergo programs are great for all size companies, even small ones. They can help employee health and company health. Yeah, it's not as easy as it looks, is it? It's a little more complex than just slipping in a CD and following the prompts. Contrary to public opinion it takes quite a bit of thinking and effort to do it right.

But several questions often pop up, along with fear, anxiety and lack of trust.

215

Questions such as;

- Should we build our own?
- Should we buy one off of Amazon?
- Is there someone who can take it over?
- How will we know it will work?
- Where do we get one?
- How do we know it's any good?
- Are they expensive?
- Etc. etc. etc.

Indeed, buying, installing, developing or establishing a company (or department) wide Ergonomics Program is similar to installing, developing or establishing a Dawg in your household.

Sometimes it's simple. It may be on a whim with your sweetheart or kids sojourning down to the local animal shelter and pick the cutest one with the big floppy ears and big puppy eyes and you are happy for the next ten years.  You got lucky, real lucky.

Image courtesy of clker.com

Maybe you inherited one from your cousin who had to move out of town. In this case like an inherited Ergo Program, you may have gotten burned with high maintenance, endless attention needs, barking at strangers, dumping on the floor, continual family complaints and chores to the point (like some programs) ownership becomes unbearable.

Maybe you found one abandoned at the local farmers market and took it home as a charity case with "Please, Please, Please," pleadings from your kids. You may have just gotten a lifetime friend who will repay you with unending benefits (like programs do) with nice warm feelings (cost savings) and knowing you helped another living creature out of pain and suffering (as a good program would).

But if you are a serious Dawg lover and want just the right Dawg, (read Ergo Program) that will affect the activities, behavior and mood of your (company) family for a significant time, you need to do your homework or due diligence.

Installing an Ergonomics program obviously takes more prep and thinking than getting a pet, but the steps are very similar. You need to do research and probably would really benefit from a *trusted* guide.

First of all if you have high expectations of a program or a pet, you have to first figure out what kind of dog / program is best for you and your (company) family.

For dogs, you go to dog shows, you talk to owners who own the breeds on your short list, get the pros and cons to determine if all the little quirks, which can develop into big full blown quirks once on-site. For instance who gets to give Fluffy their daily brushing once the newness wears off and it becomes a chore. Programs are similar.

Image courtesy of clker.com

What kind of dog do you need / want. One that doesn't bark, a small cuddly one that you can carry in your arms or a big hunting dog that doubles as a Frisbee player? Can you afford a purebred? Can you afford the maintenance (vet bills)? Will your pet / program offer you all the things you need from a pet / program like face licks or no shedding. These and many other things must be researched if you are really serious about adding a pet / program to your family.

Parameters must be set, expectations must be established, a short list made and a Franklin "T" should be done for all pros and cons. Then you seek out guidance either from a specific chosen owner, breeders and anyone else you know, because they probably know someone else who has that type of dog. In short you could very well use an experienced guide to help you through all the nuances, pros and cons, problems and benefits, trouble and happiness of owning such a dog or program.

Having a guide or resource help you in this manner will help you get a pet / install a program and have it used with great success.

DECISIONS, DECISIONS, DECISIONS

As for company wide programs, there are a bunch of them out there, with maybe a half dozen good reputable ones. But do they fit your needs? Well like dogs, you need to do your research. You have to determine how they would work inside your family / company, and for what purpose

Will your dog like everyone, is he user friendly. Is your program user friendly?

Does your dog do everything you need it to do, does it catch world class Frisbee throws, is it trainable, does your program enter, track data and show you how to make corrections?

Will your program allow you to see productivity, does it reflect cost savings, and does it do Real Ergonomics?

A company wide program should have several meaningful characteristics, among others:

- Allow fast, painless and accurate assessment
- Be user friendly for assessing and assessors
- Be able to track data
- Be able to track results
- Be able to track cost savings
- Have a correction component
- Enable data mixing and tracking across departments, sections and individuals
- Prioritize action plans
- Allow worker participation, especially in the blue collar / craft areas
- Have an accountability feature
- Have an action plan and follow-up feature
- MOST IMPORTANTLY - offer a means for solution development and be able to track those solutions

Overall, a good Ergo Program should really do what you need to be done INCLUDING both pure operations and injury prevention or solutions.

However, you have to establish how you want to do all those things before installation.

**OR**

Like dogs, you might want to look at them closely. You might listen to a knowledgeable person with a presentation of the features, costs, nuances of all the programs you know of so you have a real baseline on what kind of Ergo Program would benefit you.

Image courtesy of Graphicstock.com

At the dog show, you look around at the various dogs /programs and narrow it down. You look some more, pass the info around your family / workers / management team to evaluate acceptance or to determine what it exactly is that your family / management team needs or wants. Maybe you adopt a dog for a month to see if everyone can put up with the fleas and pooper scooping.

Some program firms allow trial installations, sometimes for free, sometimes for a small fee possibly credited towards final purchase or subscription costs. These are great for viewing programs under "battle conditions" and to see if you really can handle the time and effort, in addition to seeing the intricacies and benefits.

Like dogs, some programs are simple and easy, some are complex. And you never really know how your family or management team will adapt unless you have some research under your belt and they are tested at your home or company in real time combat conditions.

Oftentimes a program trial version is accompanied by a guide showing you all the in and outs about addressing occupational injuries, data manipulation and money saving / making, working with you throughout the trial  If so, make sure you take advantage of this and assemble lots of research for final decision.

All in all, Ergo Programs like dogs are wonderfully highly beneficial if utilized properly and continually and maintained given proper opportunity.

Essentially, your program needs to be a specific toolbox containing the tools you need to keep your company (and workers) healthy. It really is quite simple. By using your guide and doing research you should be able to customize your toolbox allowing performing really good health maintenance on your company.

Some programs are customizable specific to your needs, or perhaps you are more comfortable with something right from the box.

Image courtesy of clker.com

With this Toolbox, Can Ergo Programs Make You Money?

### *Sustainable Cost Savings? You betcha!!.*

In thinking about the all important sustainable cost savings in your own company, does Ergonomics immediately come to mind?   I'm guessing Probably NOT!! Ergonomics is generally stuck in health & safety, rarely in operations or financial departments.

Here a couple of issues really IMPACTING sustainable cost savings today:

- Absenteeism
- Turn-over or attrition
- Healthcare costs
- Operations costs

Here are a couple of eye-opening interesting tidbits about industrial injury costs:

- Total costs of Ergonomics - related injuries is estimated at $30.9 billion in the Liberty Mutual Workplace Safety Index (ErgoWeb)

- *EVERY 18 SECONDS* a worker gets a musculoskeletal disorder (MSD) including sprains, strains or back injuries (American Federation of Government Employees) – Are you one of them?

Mitigating risks and controlling costs are a top concern of employers who are only now realizing these impacts on worker health in both the white collar and blue collar / craft areas.

But who makes the decisions over programs that impact these categories? What Department? I will venture out on a limb and say that it is not Health and Safety in most organizations.

What if I tell you that an employee in pain is less productive, takes more sick days, and has a tendency to seek relief from a medical practitioner or thru a new job / tasks? Duh!

Despite the logic, with the office worker this cannot be more accurate. We know employees in discomfort take frequent breaks to seek relief. We know these employees seek medical help; when do they usually see a medical professional; during the day?  How is their morale versus an employee without discomfort?

Do you think your customers notice which one has a smile and a bit more patience?

So, what is this really costing you?   Maybe, you should measure these factors and find out.

What would a 5% increase in productivity mean for a department of 100 people?  What would a 10% decrease in absenteeism translate to for a company with 1000 employees?  What savings could you incur if 40% of your monthly doctor visits were reduced to 0?

These are some of the details you should be thinking of that can really improve your bottom line.

---

Good Ergo Programs can indeed offer sustainable cost savings in areas heretofore never even thought of, including those listed above, and this doesn't even include productivity or performance!

# A Good Example
## Of a Good Ergo Program

Here is a large insurance company dealing with, naturally insurance, insurance of all types. Obviously a vast army of Claims Managers can be found in such environs. These Claims Managers, are for the most part must operate from their seated computer workstations for the greater part of the day.

Management wanted to take steps to ensure CM health relative to the known perils of biomechanical issues at their computer workstations. After trialing and installing a good Ergo Program, guess what they found?

- A significant reduction of internal worker comp claims
- A surprising reduction in absenteeism (over 35-% in four months – tracked by the hour)

After a four month trial, the company implemented a feedback tool using Survey Monkey to see how the workers actually felt about the program. Another surprise, and totally unexpected.

An increase in overall worker morale resulted. The reason? OH MY! the clouds parted…Workers felt the company actually cared about their health and was trying to do something about it, rather than wait for the Worker Compensation system (ineffective and reactive, not proactive) to get around to it. The Ergo Program became a means for the workers to take a personal stake in information and data gathering and action plan. It allowed them to follow it through to the point of something actually being done to address their pain issues. It used to be that typically the data and information would fall on deaf ears of an assessor, hopefully trying to get something (often poorly) done attempting to alleviate symptomology.

The program provided a trackable, real time, method of data gathering and actions. The info just didn't fall into a black hole (what happens to the yellow pad notes taken by the wanna-be assessor when they dump it into the wastebasket or it gets forgotten under a pile of other assessment notes waiting for action to occur…"someday"). This accountability method also called "holding their feet to the fire" capability is a must for any good program, for without it; the "black hole" never closes and just keeps getting bigger.

A good program simply gets things done and by getting things done, it can save and generate a bunch of money.

Speaking of saving money, the company also saw a decrease in operational expense. Prior to installation it took about 5 days to get an Ergo on-site to evaluate a worker. With the program, a worker needed to only request it from management for permission to perform the self assessment and fire it in on email. It gets reviewed quickly and an action plan implemented. 48 hours is the turnaround for actual data review and action plan.

Management saw additional savings in

- No travel time for the Ergo
- Face to face scheduling eliminated
- Time for assessment is vastly decreased (long hand writing vs. short hand writing)
- Data is gathered quickly and efficiently with quick turnaround for evaluation and action plan and fully recorded for evaluation
- Workers health does not deteriorate to annoying or debilitating levels allowing efficient job performance

Yes these are ways an Ergo Program can make you money (excluding the productivity part) exemplifying sustainable cost savings.

## A GOOD COMBINATION

The main issue of most programs is that by themselves, they only offer a modicum of answers. They may show you or guide you on what to do, especially in the computer workstation environment, but for actual application, actual workstation modifications / methods changes and for some more than average problems or complex issues identified by the program, you still may need the help of a seasoned Ergo Pro who knows what they are doing, to take the program data and turn it into a real 3-dimensional solution for the workers.

Even with good data, a Bad Ergo can hinder rather than help a workstation problem identified by a good company wide program. A good program and Good Ergo combined can really help worker and company health (measured in the bottom line). Maybe you could bring in a Good Ergo to help you with an unbiased program selection.

If your program vendor is any good, they will have a high knowledge of professionals who can help you implement the solutions the program uncovers. These are the more complex ones that cannot be handled by the workers or onsite Ergo Pro.

*The most important thing here is to know the program itself is not the entire solution. You will still need the human element in addition to the data uncovered to successfully address occupational injuries.*

## Bottom Line

Like a puppy a good Ergo Program will increase morale. It will also make workers much happier knowing the company cares and offer something good for them to interact with each other and generally take ownership in some of their own healthcare and workstation modifications.

A good Ergo Program will go far to advance your worker healthcare and greatly increase overall company profitability in the form of sustained cost savings.

However, and be aware, like bad karma, a bad program will cost you money, disappointment, time and endless frustration (and do less than nothing for your workers).

*A high level of caution is strongly advised!*

# When it Comes of Time - Choose Using Great Care and Guidance!

**\*\*Don't say I didn't warn you!**

.

## Chapter X

# How to Really Help Yourself
### As an injured worker

OK Young Padawans:

Welcome to what may be for some of you, the most important part of this whole book.

## 4 Secret Super Simple Steps to REALLY help you get out of pain and back to work.

Most injured workers don't seem to realize these exist, missing out on golden opportunities for help.

The overall concept is **<u>PROVIDING SOME HELP TO YOUR DOCTOR AND GETTING YOURSELF AN ERGO EVAL</u> and eventually really getting something done for your hurt.** By now you should really understand why you need one, so we're going to show you how to get one. Right here, right now.

It's a classic "You don't know what you don't know". Nothing inherently wrong with that, you just don't know it. *Up until now, that is.*

## First of all...

You should know that it is totally uncomplicated. It doesn't take much to get it done; it doesn't even take a lot of time. It just takes knowing and application of a few little things you just never thought of before.

You hurt and you simply want to get rid of the pain whatever the doctor or chiropractor says it is. Like macho Jesse Ventura from the action movie Predator (page 135), you haven't got time for this malarkey and simply want to get on with your professional life.

You have the desire. You have the need. The only thing left is to be pointed in the right direction. Right?

Well what exactly do you do?

***Well, It Really is Quite Easy Y'All.***

See for yourself.

Simply Put, you have to take the bull by the horns and really take charge of your situation, (not your condition, two different things), be proactive and also understand why it is that no one is really helping you and why you can't look to them for answers. Understand, this will no doubt be surprising to you.

So, on with the show and the first **Super Simple Step #1**

# Super SIMPLE STEP #1

## *#1 __YOU__* Have to Take the Bull by the Horns <small>image courtesy clcker.com</small>

As an initial eye opener, in **SUPER SIMPLE STEP #1** you have to think out-of-the-box, assess your situation, take the bull by the horns, completely understand your situation and most importantly recognize….

# Why No One is Helping You!

Well, no one is helping you because ***no one knows how.*** They really don't understand why you hurt, only that you hurt, so they plainly react to treating your symptomology, not the actual cause (when it comes to workstations or work tasks being the culprit).  Not that they don't have good intentions, or don't mean well.  Not that they don't care, they just don't know how to help you probe deeper so both of you can understand the real cause of your pain and take appropriate steps to fix it.

Who is no one?  Who are they?

These folks come from your
- circle of friends
- family & loved ones
- significant others
- schoolmates
- playmates
- anyone else in your social/professional circle

What about the medical professions who are supposedly helping you?

These folks are your
- doctors & chiropractors
- physical therapists / occupational therapists
- massage therapists
- nurses & physician assistants
- doctor receptionists

That's Right! These medical professionals often don't really know what to do either. These folks, who you have been seeing, offering their learned opinions and their ongoing care giving, mostly don't have a clue when it comes to what you do for a living.

Sure they give you the benefit of all their training, schooling, and vast experience. Still they rack their brain looking for a complete solution. But by default due to time pressures and unfortunately, are generally not trained or are aware enough to delve into your work tasks causing your pain. I've seen this, time and time again. 99% of the professionals out there, only know what they know, even if they know it well, really well - expert even.

Unfortunately, this also goes for some Occupational Physicians, although, I'm pleased to note the ones that do get it, really get it or are always, always, always the first in line to ask and learn about what real Ergonomics can do.

All the medicine, physical therapy, pain, caretaking, surgeries may not get you out of pain and back to work to your chosen career or best means of livelihood for the long term, especially if they involve fixing  bad workstations or bad work tasks.

Once you complete STEP 1, taken charge and becoming aware, THAT'S GOOD.  You have just arrived at **SUPER SIMPLE STEP #2.**

## Super
## SIMPLE
## STEP
## #2

## IN SIMPLE STEP #2, you have to discover and exercise *Your Rights*

Not only do you have to take the bull by the horns, you have to "rassle" it to the ground into submission.

Image courtesy clcker.com

What comes into play here, is exercising *your rights* with full authority and when you do you will be able

to raise your hands in triumph and get back to doing what you do without pain.

THAT'S RIGHT!! You have certain undeniable rights when it comes to your own healthcare being the injured worker.

***You have the right to have a distinct say in the matter.*** The matter is of your healthcare and really addressing your pain above and beyond treatment, medications, bed rest and short term physical or occupational therapy.

Get this concept and "rassle" it to the ground and raise your hands high in the air, cry out a big YEE-HAW in knowing you are closer to that championship ring, closer to getting back to what you do without pain - Good Job!!

Too often, by virtue of awe, admiration and respect, we hold those in the medical field in high esteem and feel that whatever they say is gospel. Challenging them is not in our genetic makeup.

Well, for the most part that may be true, however there comes a time when you being the patient must stand firm and bring about a benefit with a proactive path to your own healthcare. This is especially true if it involves a workstation modification.

*TO DO THIS, YOU MUST PROVIDE SOME HELP TO YOUR DOCTOR.*

<u>Let me repeat that, since it is vitally important.</u>

***YOU MUST PROVIDE SOME HELP TO YOUR DOCTOR****. – Become part of his team, and you know what? He'll love you for it.* You will probably be opening their eyes into a completely new world.

You must gently, but firmly or assertively prod them into doing what is right for you. You have to help them see the light, with the workstation, work tasks, or big picture, not just your symptomologies. You must guide the discussion to workstation or work task elements. *<u>You have to generate this part of the conversation.</u>*

## *Current scenarios often go like this:*

Doctors prescribe some physical therapy and rest or some manipulation treatment, often followed by some form of work hardening (in many ways a slow purposeful integration to get you back to work, generally to the same work tasks that injured you in the first place). The downside is, after an injury, and after all this treatment, you go back to a job or workstation that is the problem in the first place, and B-I-N-G-O:

*You get injured all over again.*

By now having completed **STEPS #1 & #2**, determining you do not want to return to an injury causing workstation, you are now at the point of knowing what to tell your doctor what it is that you think would help. Kudos to you! You have successfully arrived at **SUPER SIMPLE STEP #3**

# Super
# SIMPLE
# STEP
# #3

# SIMPLE STEP #3 is getting your healthcare provider to recommend or prescribe, on paper, an Ergonomics Analysis.

*A What??*

***An Ergo Analysis or Ergo Assessment.***

**That's it!! That's all there is to it.** Naturally there are a couple of minor but important details to be aware of.

Nowadays, doctors routinely order up Physical Capacity Evaluations (PCE), Independent Medical

Examinations (IME), Work Hardening / Occupational Therapy (OT), Physical Therapy (PT), all to address specific injuries. Rarely do they ever offer up an Ergo Eval. It is actually quite easily done. It's just like ordering up all that other treatment. You just have to bring up the subject.

## *MOST IMPORTANTLY...*

**You have to ensure they call out an Ergonomics Assessment or Analysis for you. And if they don't know why, you have to be prepared to justify why, by whom and the benefits for you.**

**This is because they rarely prescribe an Ergonomics Assessment or Analysis. Again, I know, I've seen it literally hundreds of times. Even many Occupational Physicians (their self moniker is Ock Docs) don't fully understand what real Ergonomic Applications or Workstation Modifications can do to address symptomology and reduce injury, although they are usually the most receptive.**

It's not necessarily that they don't want to. It's just something they don't usually do and it is not an auto reflex for an industrial injury. You would think Occupational Physicians would be cognizant of industrial solutions. Sadly, I have seen, they are not. If you have found one that is, keep him. He's worth his weight in gold.

So you, being the injured worker must "take the bull by the horns" and prod your medical professional to actually dictate this subject in the form of a prescription or chart note letter allowing you the path to correct a workstation.

## *If you don't do it then probably no one will.*

*So here it is:*
*A very important albeit*
*A NOT SO Well Known*
*Injured Workers Right*

Actually, this should be a well known right of the injured worker. The ability to elicit from their primary caregiver this simple phrase.

*"Ergonomics Assessment of*
*Workstation Required"*
*by*
*Professional Ergonomist*
*(Certified if available)*
*With*
*Follow-up by Physician*
*(to determine effectiveness)*

To get this in writing on a physician form, ***YOU SIMPLY HAVE TO ASK***. It is well within your right and ***YOU*** are then helping your physician in your own healthcare since his primary goal is to take care of ***YOU*** and if you give him this little gem then the both of you are fully vested in your care.

Now both of you have a weapon with which to fight injury and _**YOU**_ are the beneficiary in winning that war against pain.

For the most part you will be pleasantly surprised at the support you get from your physician. Secretly, they often look for any help they can get in your healthcare and in fact will welcome your input, especially if it reaches across an area they are unfamiliar with. This is also true if it is easy for them to "get the ball rolling" in the right direction to get you out of pain. I know, I've seen this too! It's what they signed up and took that Hippocratic Oath for.

BUT REMEMBER, _**YOU**_ have to bring it up. _**You**_ have to understand what Ergonomics can do for you. Relay this to your doctor and have them _write that prescription._

Then of course, once you have this prescription, it will be up to _**YOU**_ to find a competent Ergo Professional and not succumb to a Voodoo Ergonomist. This may be the most difficult part of the super secret step stuff. By having read Chapter II (State-Of-The Art) I'm sure you re aware of voodoo types out there. Go to great lengths to avoid them!

Finding one of course brings us to **Super Simple Step #4.**

# Super
# SIMPLE
# STEP
# #4

## #4. <u>YOU</u> have to find not only a good but competent Ergonomist because your doctor generally won't know one. This may be the hardest of the 4 super simple steps.

Never fear. I have enclosed an excellent article penned by my friend Ms. Alison Heller-Ono PT, CPE of Worksite International on how to distinguish between the many different "Alphabet Soup," certifications of the various practitioners.

I'm sure you will be surprised at the differences and how some can falsely hide behind some letters, misrepresenting themselves. Of course you can easily see what happens if you mistakenly retain the improper one for your indusrial injury project.

This article is an excellent guide on how to find a real Ergonomist specific to your needs and offers detailed descriptions of what separates the various practitioner types.

Alison is a dynamite lady. She is also uniquely both a trained Physical Therapist and Certified Professional Ergonomist, allowing her to approach and analyze Ergonomic projects from the anatomical / medical viewpoint and also from a task performance angle. She has a heart of gold, knows her stuff and has a wonderful sense of humor combined with a great smile.

Her take on the charlatans is similar to my own, and in scribing this book, I'm finding more and more high level pros are put off a bit by those lacking in skillsets actually not helping people, even making injured workers worse and damaging reputations.

Alison's article should lead you in the right direction. Give her a call sometime. She always, always has time to discuss Ergonomics.
You can find her at:

## www.worksiteinternational.com
## 888.288.4463

Ms. Heller-Ono's article from her website is reproduced in its entirety in the Appendix, page 273

Alison has a different name for the voodooists
She calls them carpetbaggers
See her article to find out why.

Dwg-wikipedia.com

Congratulations!! You've made it this far and can see the prize trophy. Now it is up to you to implement these 4 Super Secret Simple Steps.

*Copy this page, cut it out and pin it up in your office. Or carry it in your wallet or use it for a bookmark in your favorite detective novel. Do this and you are well on your way to Really Helping Yourself!*

"Cut along this line ↓--- **Tear out sheet also on P.299**

# 4 Super Secret Simple Steps Summary

Here are the four steps summarized with a bit of advice to really helping yourself in dealing with your workplace injury.

1. Understand & take charge of your situation – bull by the horns thing

2. Exercising your rights – "rassle" that concept down and show who's boss

3. Help out your physician and show him how to write a prescription – he'll welcome your help and input, and believe me, you will be helping him do his job in your healthcare

4. The hardest part may be in finding a good, I mean really good Ergo you can believe in, trust and know they will and can take care of you. Alison's article in the Appendix will help you take care of that.

**HERE ARE A COUPLE OF EXTRA DETAILS TO REMEMBER** and apply appropriately.

To get an Ergonomics Evaluation ***YOU*** simply have to ask your physician (or other med pro) to write it down. It's that effortless. Occasionally the physicians will tell you they will leave it up to the claims manager or insurance company (without any prodding or suggestion) and hope they will do the "right thing." Be assured that these folks are generally "in the dark" just like all the other folks listed above and probably won't know what the "right thing" is. *You* may have to go to bat for yourself against this additional front, but its well worth the effort.

Once ***YOU*** have the Ergo prescription, you now have a legal "weapon" with which to further your case with the worker comp, insurance or HR folks. They should listen. It's a legal document and packs a lot of punch. It's your secret weapon. But like any weapon, you have to use it correctly to have any real effect. Take care not to shoot yourself in the foot. Lots and lots of follow up is not uncommon, be prepared.

But be assured, even with this secret weapon, it really is up to ***YOU*** to stand up for yourself and professionally or gently prod your medical professional or claims manager, or whoever, to advocate for ***YOU*** to help you get your workstation or work tasks changed to get your pain eliminated.

After all, if **_YOU_** don't do it, chances are no one else will, or they may (un)intentionally put a lot of roadblocks in your way.

## Case Example

Here is a typical successful scenario when someone took the bull by the horns and followed Super Secret Simple Steps 1-4. Pain is reduced, symptomology abated, professional work tasks can be again efficiently performed pain free and professional life can be pleasant once again.

Our injured worker was a legal assistant and computer jockey in a big law firm spending hours and hours at breakneck speeds inputting data onto a computer in addition to lots and lots of filing.

The hours keyboarding took its toll on her wrists and forearms. Filing in the large 4 drawer lateral files crammed full of Pendaflex folders pushed her shoulder symptomologies over the edge. Both areas developed intolerable pain.

The doctors advice: Change jobs, slow down, find other things to do, take lots and lots of breaks, get someone else to help you out, and by the way here some oxycodone (just for the short term tho'- we don't want you getting addicted now do we?)

Well, she blew through all the typical recommendations, PT,OT meds and surprise,

surprise, her symptomology still flared to higher levels, especially her shoulders from the filing.

Have you tried to pull a series of legal files from a crammed full lateral file lately? It does indeed blow out your shoulders, especially when the high level drawers are packed to the brim with files. Here you've got extended reach, pulling to a position over your head and using muscles in the most inefficient manner known to man. Plus you have to use severe pinch grip since the files are usually really tough to pull up and out, being packed in close to each other like sardines.

Fortunately, we were doing some expert testimony for a senior partner and he told her to contact us to see if there was anything to do for alleviating her pain that had been ongoing for a few years.

We performed an intake and took her through all four of the Super Secret Simple Steps 1-4

A prescription was made, gathered and presented to the claims manager, who then and only then authorized an Ergo assessment.

The assessment documented all analysis, observations, conclusions and showed standard ergo type changes for her specific biomechanicals, but also to develop some super secret office tools to help with her staple removing and Pentaflex file pulling. Of special note was that the tools designed were presented (and approved) in the analysis to the CM being part of the design sequence actually addressing the specific tasks triggering her pain. The CM was really interested in closing the claim.

As the project closed up, we presented a closing report to the physician complete with photos of the modified workstation work tasks, special tools and documented the benefits and injured worker's testimony.

Not surprisingly they sound a lot like Ellie B's testimony in Chapter VI Success Stories, and like Ellie B. the project was quite successful.

Since the doctors saw how workstation modifications could successfully address patient pain, we now occasionally receive referrals from them, since they now know of our work and how we are now part of their patients care team.

It's nice to be appreciated. She still works for the law firm, in a lot less pain and more task efficient.

No matter what the job. From computer jockey to a factory assembly worker to maintenance worker to bulldozer operator to landscaper, the **Super Secret Simple Steps 1-4** will prove totally effective.

## You've got the plan, now it's up to you to take these final steps and really put yourself on the path to recovery

Don't settle for simply managing the symptomology, get rid of the injury entirely and get on with your life.

### *It's that simple.*

Like Nike says **"Just Do It!"**

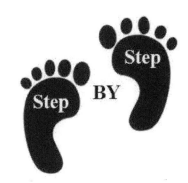

## An interesting end note:

Once this methodology began to take form, I found that many professionals involved with Ergo (safety managers, Ergo Pros, HR, among others) agreed with me and wished more injured workers would become more self aware of their rights. If this happened then the injured workers would lobby and advocate for themselves and come from a stronger and more knowledgeable position rather than leaving it to the other organizational personages to figure things out for managing their care.

*It would certainly take a big load off the folks responsible for moving the claim, help the medical professionals and make life a lot better for all workers in pain.*

Like the physicians, these other pros would welcome the help, because it essentially makes their job easier and in the same vein helps you with better health care. So both sides have a mutual benefit. I found it most pleasurable that other health care professionals shared this view point.

## Chapter XI
# In Conclusion

With these writings and thoughts, I give you my most outrageous stories and some of my most trade secrets. Hopefully, you found them instructive, inspirational, enlightening, humorous and valuable.

You've seen what benefits Real Ergonomics can do and the damage Voodoo Ergonomics can also do.

I charter you to take this knowledge and

Go Forth to:

- Make Ergonomics a real accepted and valued science
- Help those with serious injuries craft their future
- Improve peoples lives
- Take it upon yourself to do something no other can

You now have the knowledge and power to:

- Really help people
- Impact their lives
- Take away their pain
- Help secure their future

And do you know what that's worth?

Like the credit card commercial says:

It's priceless… and it will bestow upon you the knowledge that you can do something for someone, that few others can or are capable of which in itself is a marvelous reward.

> *Don't let this marvelous science languish in a sea of mistrust, misunderstanding and misuse.*
>
> *Take it and help mature it to the highest level it can be.*

As Jean Luc Picard was so fond of saying

## *"Make it so"*

# APPENDIX

# A
# Definition
# of
# Ergonomics

# A Definition of Ergonomics - con't

Ergonomics is a complex science, so much so that it currently defies a real definitive definition (how's that???) understandable and applicable to the everyday Joe.  Depending on who you talk to in the street you will get a different answer from the query "What do you think Ergonomics is?

As many people think it is different things they all have kind of an ethereal understanding of its applications and nuances, however few ever get it right.

For your reading and educational pleasure, I proffer several definitions.  All have merit and the most complete I feel is the one crafted by the International Ergonomics Association.

### ər-gə-'na-'mik-s - *adj*

Obviously, the definitions vary according to one's own knowledge of understanding and interpretation. To wit, even many of the dictionaries abound with differing definitions.  Go ahead ask anyone what Ergonomics is…and you'll get:  it's a uhhh…umm…ahhh…well it's ……see Chapter II. It seems dictionaries have the same problem.

# A Definition of Ergonomics - con't

## So, here's one simple definition.

*Safer, more productive work tasks
and workstations*

Complete, succinct and the average worker can
relate to and understand it, also immediately relating
what it can do for them.

---

All right, all right, for those who would like a more
distinct definition, how's this, from pagaday.com,
workman publishing:

**ur-gho-nom'-ik-x** - *adj*: *designed or arranged
for safe, comfortable, and efficient use. The science
of designing and arranging things people use so that
the people and things interact most efficiently and
safely.* (Author's note; the definition should say
***efficient human use***, with the definition being
mangled, to wit; see the Ergonomic dog toys in
another chapter).

It is kind of a banal definition; it really leaves me
kind of flat. Totally uninteresting and stated in a
manner that really doesn't show potential,
application or how really beneficial the science can
be.

# A Definition of Ergonomics - con't

Here is another, from Wikipedia no less
*Human factors and ergonomics (HF&E), also known as comfort design, functional design, and user-friendly systems, is the practice of designing products, systems or processes to take proper account of the interaction between them and the people that use them.*

Not a word about safety and/or occupational injury.

Still a little incomplete and unsatisfied?

---

*Here is probably one of, if not THE best definition, directly from the*

## IEA, (International Ergonomics Association).
www.iea.cc

The IEA is essentially a group of 42 federated societies from around the world, and is a wonderful support group for any and all things Ergonomic.

If you are some kind of aspiring Ergo, Please, Please support them and at least visit their web page for more details. They really are doing wonderful things for the profession.

# A Definition of Ergonomics - con't

Here's the IEA agreed definition of Ergonomics (2000)

*Ergonomics helps harmonizing things that interact with people in terms of people's needs, abilities and limitations.*

*Derived from the Greek ergon (work) and nomos (laws) to denote the science of work, ergonomics is a systems-oriented discipline which now extends across all aspects of human activity. Practicing ergonomists must have a broad understanding of the full scope of the discipline. That is, ergonomics promotes a holistic approach in which considerations of physical, cognitive, social, organizational, environmental and other relevant factors are taken into account. Ergonomists often work in particular economic sectors or application domains. Application domains are not mutually exclusive and they evolve constantly; new ones are created and old ones take on new perspectives.*

*There exist domains of specialization within the discipline, which represent deeper competencies in specific human attributes or characteristics of human interaction.*

*Domains of specialization within the discipline of ergonomics are broadly the following:*

- *Physical Ergonomics*
- *Cognitive Ergonomics*
- *Organizational Ergonomics*

*Visit the IEA website for more detailed info on these domains of specialization. And support the organizations good work whenever and however you can.*

# A Definition of Ergonomics - con't

**Author's note about definitions:**

It seems that the science of Ergonomics is quickly expanding to include the many aspects of human life and tasks. Therefore a single complete definition may not be easily forthcoming.

The IEA definition, although lengthy, is this way simply to include the many various elements that the overall term Ergonomics encompasses. It may also be that the (your) definition might also just be limited to the specific application or project you are working on or involved with, which would be very valid in its own right.

Such as;

- Computer Ergonomics
- Tool Ergonomics
- Chair Ergonomics
- Psychosocial Ergonomics
- Or Whatever

Naturally these valued definitions include many areas of Ergonomics of which the casual reader or user may not be aware of and which aspects are well beyond the scope of this book.

# A Definition of Ergonomics - con't

However, their inclusion may inspire some to perhaps follow their path and help advance the science.

And maybe when the term Ergonomics is bantered about in fancy dinner parties, the first question phrased should be:

> *"And exactly what kind of Ergonomics are we talking about?"*

This would really help the definition center itself in good conversation and help in being clearer in the minds of those using the word, having a vested interest in it, and especially within the thinking of those who would benefit by its applications.

# Deciphering the Alphabet Soup of Ergonomics Certifications

Alison Heller-Ono PT CPE – Worksite International

# Deciphering the Alphabet Soup Of Ergonomics Certifications

Alison Heller-Ono PT CPE – Worksite International

CPE, AEP, CIE, CAE. CEES, CEAS I, II, III, COEE. What do they all mean to or for you?

*Believe me, they are all immensely different!*

"**Caveat Emptor**" or buyers beware fits well when employers are selecting ergonomics service providers. The phrase arises from buyers often having less information about the services they are purchasing than the seller is revealing to them. Buyers of ergonomics services often don't necessarily understand the science of ergonomics, what makes a good ergonomics consultant, the differences in their education, training and experiences which impacts the quality of service provided and ultimately the results the buyer or employer will achieve. These days, ergonomic credentials and certifications are **like a bowl of alphabet soup**, and totally confusing to buyers.

When it comes to ergonomic service providers, employers and insurers should be aware of the many credentials ergonomic specialists are putting after their name. There are vast differences in the credentials and certifications offered in today's marketplace resulting in significant differences in skills, experience, knowledge, and of course deliverables. *In addition, many folks perceive (office) ergonomics as something "easy" to do as a startup business, or add-on service.* In reality, this is a professional career path requiring substantial education and training not everyone is suited for.

Many ergonomics service providers are simply modern-day "carpetbaggers, exploiting and profiteering from the misfortune or confusion of others.
Image courtesy Wikipedia.com / carpetbaggers

To some extent, the current state of ergonomics is reflective of United States history, when Northern **carpetbaggers** moved to the South after the American Civil War, in order to profit from the instability and power vacuum that existed at this time. Following the 1997 Cal-OSHA ergonomics regulation and the push for better health and wellness in the workplace, sit to stand trends in the office and other legislative changes supporting individual's abilities to work without pain, ergonomics services have become extremely popular and competitive, especially in California.

Matching the right ergonomics professional to your needs is critical when you are designing a new technical process in an assembly line or production area, setting up an ergonomics process for your organization, or returning an injured worker with a medical condition back to work to assure a successful outcome. Employers need to be sure they engage with a **certified professional ergonomics consultant** who is able to perform a valid ergonomics analysis, recommend and implement appropriate solutions for the desired results.

Who is your consultant? Your bearer of knowledge? They could be a:

- Chiropractor
- Loss control agent
- Local furniture vendor
- Physical or Occupational therapist
- Occupational health nurse
- Administrative Assistant
- Facilities manager
- Safety manager or technician
- Office supply store representative
- Ergonomic product salesman

*Knowing who your ergonomics service provider is critical. But beware they may be lacking in the appropriate credentialing and by association appropriate skillsets.*

## Let's Clear the Air

With so many people **_"dabbling"_** in ergonomics, it's time to clear up all the confusion. Aside from earning a Master's Degree in Human Factors and Ergonomics, there are no state or national criteria or licensing body at this time to credential Ergonomists.  Fortunately, there are **nationally recognized board certification organizations (non-profit) or privately held, "for profit" credentialing businesses.  However, not all are trustworthy as noted in the following charts.**

Ergonomics is an applied science, so people with degrees in healthcare, engineering, psychology and other non-degreed backgrounds can be certified.  Here's a comparison of some current obtainable credentials.  Suffice to say that a close review will help you when it comes time to retain the most appropriate service provider for your project.

## Not-for-Profit Institutions Offering Certification Programs

| Organization | Type | Certification | Criteria for Certification | Training length in lieu of degree or experience to obtain Certification |
|---|---|---|---|---|
| **BCPE** Board of Certification in Professional Ergonomics *not-for-profit* $159 app fee $350 exam fee $150 annual fee | National Board Certification | **CPE** - *Certified Professional Ergonomist* | **CPE** Bachelor degree with appropriate course work 3 years experience Pass 8 hour valid exam 2 work samples (analysis, design) | |
| | | **AEP** - *Associate Ergonomics Professional* | **AEP** Bachelor degree with appropriate course work Requires < 3 years experience Pass 4 hour valid exam | |
| | | **CEA** - *Certified Ergonomics Associate* | DISCONTINUED | |
| http://www.bcpe.org | | | | |

# Deciphering the Alphabet Soup of
## Ergonomics Certifications – con't

**Not-for-Profit Institutions Offering Certification Programs - con't**

| Organization | Type | Certification | Criteria for Certification | Training length in lieu of degree or experience to obtain Certification |
|---|---|---|---|---|
| **ORI** Oxford Research Institute *not-for-profit* $475 app fee $130 annual fee | National Board Certification | **CIE -** *Certified Industrial Ergonomist* | **CIE** -BS or BA degree 4 yr experience in ergonomics 2-3 qualitative work samples 2 letters of recommendations 85% score on written exam | |
| | | **CAE -** *Certified Associate Ergonomist* | **CAE** BS or BA degree 1 yr experience in ergonomics 1 letter of recommendation 1 work sample 70% score on 2.5 hr exam | |
| http://www.oxfordresearch.org/cert_program.htm | | | | |
| **OSHA** *not-for-profit* $24.95 one time fee | U.S. Federal Government | **OSHA** *OSHA Training Inst. Education Center Certificate of Completion* | **NONE REQUIRED** $24.95 one time fee | 1 Hour on-line course Up to 6 months for completion |
| http://www.usfosha.com/ergonomics-certificate.aspx | | | | |

271

## For-Profit Private Businesses Offering Certification Programs

| Organization | Type | Certification | Criteria for Certification | Training length in lieu of degree or experience to obtain Certification |
|---|---|---|---|---|
| MATHESON'S Ergonomic Evaluation Certification *for profit* | Private Business Certification | CEES - *Certified Ergonomic Evaluation Specialist* | NONE REQUIRED $1,450 per training session | Attend 4 day training by Matheson On-line test score of 85% Submit 2 office ergo evals Recertification required after 5 yr |
| http://www.roymatheson.com | | | | |
| BACK SCHOOL OF ATLANTA *for profit* | Private Business Certification | CEAS I, II, III - *Certified Ergonomic Assessment Specialist* | NONE REQUIRED $350 one time fee | CEAS I - 2 day workshop (on-line or live) CEAS II, III Advanced Training No additional criteria noted |
| http://www.thebackschool.net | | | | |
| OCCUPRO *for profit* | Private Business Certification | COEE - *Certified Office Ergonomic Evaluator* | NONE REQUIRED $300 - on demand $350 - in class / live webcast | 1 day training (live or on-demand) Submit 5 evaluations Peer review |
| http://www.occupro.net/education/continuing-education/office-ergonomics/ | | | | |

**For-Profit Private Businesses Offering Certification Programs - con't**

| Organization | Type | Certification | Criteria for Certification | Training length in lieu of degree or experience to obtain Certification |
|---|---|---|---|---|
| Emergency University *for profit* | Private Business Certification | Certificate for Ergonomics On line Training Completion | NONE REQUIRED $39.95 one time fee | 40 minute on-line training program Teaches self assessment of your own computer workstation Not for assessing others |
| http://www.emergencyuniversity.com/ergonomics | | | | |
| Music Ergonomics LLC *for profit* | Private Business Certification | Certificate in Transformational Ergonomics | NONE REQUIRED $550.00 one time fee | Home Study course One person class module of 15 hours Add'l mentoring @ $20 / half hour |
| https://laurierileymusic.wordpress.com/music-ergonomist-training-program/ | | | | |
| ErgoConsulting (Canada) | Private Business Certification | Certificate of Course Completion | NONE REQUIRED $599 one time fee for ea workshop | 1 Day Workshop Conduct Ergonomic Risk Assessments 1 Day Workshop Office Ergonomic Assessments 1 Day Workshop Physical Demands Assessments |
| https://www.ergoconsulting.ca/ergonomic-training-services/public-workshops/ | | | | |

# Deciphering the Alphabet Soup of
## Ergonomics Certifications – con't

## Educational Institutions Offering Certification Programs

| Organization | Type | Certification | Criteria for Certification | Training length in lieu of degree or experience to obtain Certification |
|---|---|---|---|---|
| University of Fredericton On-line format (Canada) | Educational Institution | Certificate of Course Completion for Ergonomics Coordinator | NONE REQUIRED $1920 full tuition for for both courses | 2 courses @ 8 weeks ea Foundations course Advanced course |
| http://www.ufred.ca/ergonomics-coordinator-certificate/ | | | | |
| New York University (NYU) Langone Medical Center | Educational Institution | Adv. Certificate Program in Ergonomics | BA degree in IE or similar | 12 credit hours of course work GRE testing $1,554 per credit tuition 12 x $1,554 = $18,646 full tuition |
| http://oioc.med.nyu.edu/education/certificate/ | | | | |
| Simon Fraser University (Canada) | Educational Institution | Certificate of Course Completion in Occupational Ergonomics Program | Enrollment in concurrent undergraduate program required | 8 Ergo courses of 3 credits ea. req'd Other undergraduate courses as req'd $654.94 / credit - U.S. residence $173.91 / credit - Canada residence |
| https://www.sfu.ca/bpk/news_events/news/occupationalergonomicscertificate.html | | | | |
| Colorado State U (on line format) | Educational Institution | Certificate of Course Completion | NONE REQUIRED | 3 major units / 30 modules 6 month time limit $395 full tuition $25 admin fee |
| http://www.online.colostate.edu/certificates/ergonomics/ | | | | |

# Deciphering the Alphabet Soup of Ergonomics Certifications – con't

## Educational Institutions Offering Certification Programs - con't

| Organization | Type | Certification | Criteria for Certification | Training length in lieu of degree or experience to obtain Certification |
|---|---|---|---|---|
| Penn State U | Educational Institution | *Grad. Certificate In Human Factors Engineering & Ergonomics* | BA or BS degree in IE or similar | 3 courses req'd @ 3 cr. ea plus 4 prerequsit req'd @ 3 cr. ea $790 per credit = $16,590 total tuition |
| http://www.worldcampus.psu.edu/degrees-and-certificates/human-factors-engineering-ergonomics-certificate/overview | | | | |
| University of Central Florida UCF | Educational Institution | *Grad. Certificate in Industrial Ergonomics & Safety* | BA or BS degree in IE or similar | 12 credit hours of course work 4 courses of 3 credits ea $288 /credit x 12 = $3,456 full tuition |
| http://www.graduatecatalog.ucf.edu/programs/program.aspx?id=1252 | | | | |
| University of Utah School of Medicine COSH program (on line format) | Educational Institution | *Grad. Certificate in Occpational Safety & Health* | BA or BS degree | 17 credits of Ergo & Safety courses $1,593 / 1 credit hr $2563 / 3 credit hrs $6940 / 12 credit hrs |
| http://medicine.utah.edu/rmcoeh/education-degrees/graduate-certificate-occupational-safety-health/ergonomics-safety.php) | | | | |

Becoming certified is evidence of a minimum level of professional competence, but also beware that **demonstrating the necessary competence has significant variability depending on the credential selected**

Years of experience, education level and ergonomics work experience separate a CPE from a CEAS or COEE. While certification is important to advance the credibility of a profession, employers should be mindful of what each credential brings and match it appropriately to their ergonomic needs.

*When comparing and selecting an ergonomics service provider, be sure to select the most qualified and experienced professional needed for your ergonomics project to assure the most successful outcome.*

*Be wary of the "alphabet soup" of "ergonomics carpetbaggers".*

*Worksite International's ergonomics services are provided by highly trained, experienced and qualified professionals credentialed with the highest level of certification possible with an accompanying healthcare degree. We are qualified to support employers through the continuum of work health care from wellness to prevention to medical workers' compensation and disability matters.*

# A
# Collection
# Of
# Voodoo
# Ergonomic
# Things

# For Your Amusement & Amazement

A collection of things Ergonomic  ___NOT!___

**These things are called Ergonomic for who knows what reason other than the charlatan makers are talking stories to push their product onto unsuspecting buyers who might think these devices are higher quality, better, more valuable or easier to use.**
**(See Chapter IV Snake Oil Ergonomics).**

**It's just a marketing ploy!**

_**Please don't be duped by**_
_**The Hype.**_

Mostly they elicit the reaction of:
"You've GOT to be Kidding Me!"

If it says it's Ergonomic on the packaging, it probably isn't and they're trying to snow you!!!!

Sorta like advertising saying
"Organic", or "Green" or "Revolutionary"
_Or get this_ "All Natural."

# Voodoo Ergonomic Things – con't

Hunter Fan 56" Brushed Nickel Ergonomic Ceiling Fan

This Brushed Nickel Ergonomic fan from Hunter is a solid contemporary fan, great to brighten any room. It comes with a remote to make using it, a breeze. This model moves air quietly and so efficiently in fact it is backed by Hunter's limited lifetime warranty. Hunter Ceiling Fans have been energy

(http://www.sears.com/search=Hunter%20Ergonomic %2056%20in%20Brushed%20Nickel%20Ceiling%20Fan)

(http://www.lyst.com/clothing/zara-ergonomic-bermuda-shorts-with-belt-navy-blue/)

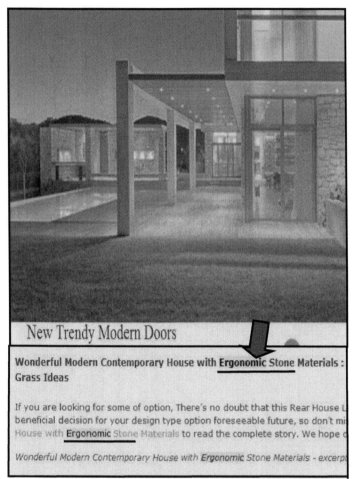

New Trendy Modern Doors

**Wonderful Modern Contemporary House with Ergonomic Stone Materials :
Grass Ideas**

If you are looking for some of option, There's no doubt that this Rear House L
beneficial decision for your design type option foreseeable future, so don't mi
House with **Ergonomic** Stone Materials to read the complete story. We hope o

*Wonderful Modern Contemporary House with Ergonomic Stone Materials - excerpt*

Even Architects are getting into the swing of things calling
structural materials as "Ergonomic Stone Materials". I have
never seen an Ergonomic Stone and I wish an Architect would
show me some.

(http://www.biawow.com/wonderful-modern-contemporary-
house-with-ergonomic-stone-materials/rear-house-landscape-
design-swimming-pool-open-yard-green-grass-ideas/)

Belts don't need to be Ergonomic since its purpose is to hold up the pants and isn't handled a lot – It's like saying a bungee cord is Ergonomic
http://www.snickersworkwear.com/products/
accessories/belts/ergonomic-belt/

Pants also don't need to be Ergonomic, unless you might have four legs or something - fashion and styling should not be confused with Ergonomics
(http://www.revzilla.com/motorcycle/
scott-ergonomic-tp-rain-pants)

# Voodoo Ergonomic Things – con't

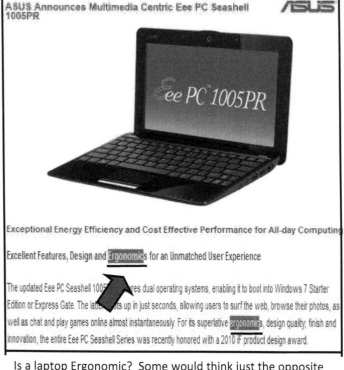

Is a laptop Ergonomic? Some would think just the opposite
(http://hothardware.com/News/ASUS-Announces-Multimedia-Centric-Eee-
PC-Seashell-1005PR/)

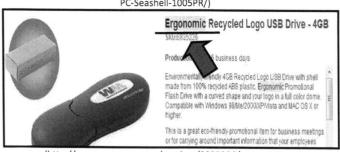

(http://www.epromos.com/product/8835236/ergonomic-
recycled-logo-usb-drive.html)

Doesn't this bench REEK of Ergonomics?
(http://www.wayfair.com/Decoteak-Outdoor-Teak-Ergonomic-
Bench-Storage-Shelf-or-Table-DT109B-DECO1004.html)

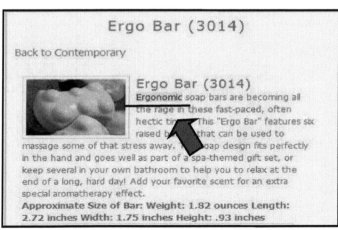

When the bumps melt away is it still Ergo?
(http://www.flexusmolds.com/3014.html)

# Voodoo Ergonomic Things – con't

MINIMALIST ERGONOMIC FIREPLACE DESIGNS

Modern Fireplace

nu-flame.com

Ventless Bio Ethanol Fireplaces Modern
Fireplaces for Anywhere!

(http://www.iroonie.com/minimalist-ergonomic-fireplace-designs/)

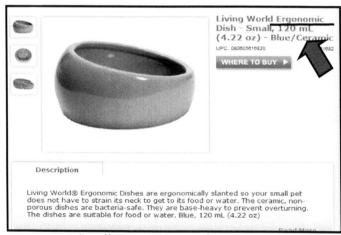

(http://www.entirelypets.com/living-world-
ergonomic-dish-blue-small.html)

# Voodoo Ergonomic Things – con't

## Bottle design: 85-year-old beer has a modern, ergonomic bottle

-- *Packaging Digest, 2/1/2008 2:00:00 AM*

SAB Miller's updated bottle design for Cristal, which the company claims the number-one-selling beer in Peru already, is expected to increase sales to 590 million liters in 2007 from 450 million liters in 2006. The brand, which has been in the Peruvian market for 85 years, now sports four versions of a redesigned amber -glass bottle: a 1.1-L returnable bottle, a 650-mL returnable bottle, a 330-mL returnable bottle and a 330-mL nonreturnable bottle.

The bottles are manufactured by O-I (www.o-i.com), designed to make consumption a better experience for its consumers. "When developing the concept, we first had to clearly understand the Cristal consumer needs and personality," says Fernando Melgar, brand manager for Cervecer as Peruanas Backus y Johnston, SAB Miller, Latam. "Then, we determined that the bottle design had to be well defined and both gregarious and ergonomic. In addition, the consumer needed to be able to grab two or three bottles at a time, while still having a good bottle/size impression."

SAB Miller also launched its first flint-glass beer bottle for Barena, aimed at the Peruvian market. "Barena is a refreshing beer that targets the growing young adult market," explains SAB Miller Barena Brand Manager Per Bernardo Leon. Barena's 650-mL returnable, 330-mL returnable 330-mL nonreturnable bottles are flint-glass and also made by O-I. They're said to keep the product colder for a more enjoyable drinking experience.

(http://www.packagingdigest.com/packaging-design/bottle-design-85-year-
old-beer-has-modern-ergonomic-bottle)

No comment!
(Author's Collection)

# Voodoo Ergonomic Things – con't

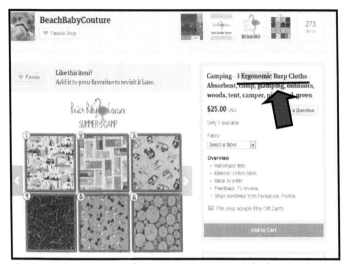

Every new parent needs an Ergonomic Burp Cloth – Available
in assorted colors and patterns"
http://www.BeachBabyC.com

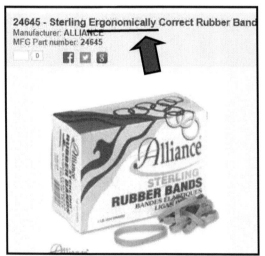

Ergonomically correct rubber bands for every
Ergonomically correct office

# Voodoo Ergonomic Things – con't

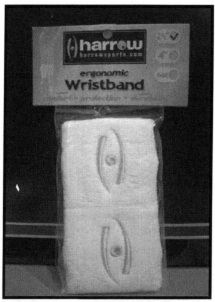

Is your wrist Ergonomic?
(Author's Collection)

Even cats need Ergonomics – Don't all animals?
(http://www.overstock.com/Pet-Supplies/Pet-Pals-Acoustic-
Ergonomic-Design-Cool-Guitar-Cat-House/6294145/product.html)

# Voodoo Ergonomic Things – con't

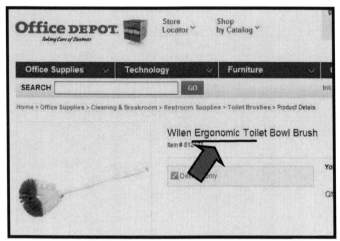

Ever needed to clean your Ergonomic Toilet Bowl?
(http://www.officedepot.com/a/products/812471/Wilen-Ergonomic-Toilet-Bowl-Brush/)

http://www.theklipstik.com/

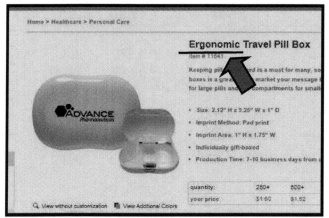

Where to put your Ergonomic pills?
http://promotions.advanceweb.com/Personal-Care/11641-Customized-
Wholesale-Ergonomic-Travel-Pill-Box.aspx

Got one, a
favorite we could
maybe
include in our next
book?
Let us know!

More to Come!!

# Thanks & Send us an Email

Thanks for being part of our Ergonomics world. I hope you have at least laughed, were entertained or were inspired and made some discoveries of your own.

If so, I would really love to hear about it (absurd or not). Maybe you would like feedback on one of your projects or just want to gab about Ergonomics like Ellie B, in Chapter IV.

We would love to hear your feedback on our and your adventures.

Give us a poke if you would like to know more about Real Ergonomists and their work!!!

ian@ergoinc.com
www.ergoinc.com
<open invitation to mentee wannabes>

Meanwhile, practice some Serious Ergonomics and make a positive impact on someone's life. Become someone they will thank. You will be a much better person for it. You will also make the world a better place.

***I truly believe that.***

# Acknowledgements

In addition to those respectably listed in the front page dedications, I gratefully acknowledge the following folks who have provided insight, critique, friendship, inspiration and company in my pursuit of completing this Ergonomic Adventure. Without whose help and friendship, I truly would not have been able to hit the finish line. My sincerest thanks go to them and my apologies to those I have inadvertently left out. However, you know who you are and undoubtedly will never cease to forever give me grief reminding me of that.

I offer my thanks, raise a glass and give a tip o' the hat to these folks for their wonderful contributions, listed in no particular order: Erwin T., Sillikins, Lance P., Hannah S., Julie L., Mac-in-on, Lexi C., Jilli Bean, Paul A., Ojo, Andy I., Rough Tough, Jiminy James, The Susan, Sue Ro., AAAAron, Jeff R., Jeffie J., Joanne B., Scotty, Cracker, Susan Ha., Joy S., Wayne M., Brian D., Sabrina S., Steve Mo., Susan T., Miriam J., Paul S., Gordonzo, Carrie G-W., Bowman, Pace, Peter B., Alison HO., Diana G., Sue Anne, Jon B., Teddy Bear, Ritus, Loren A., Josh R., John C., Tagler, Maggy B., Ira J., Sailer, Hector, Wilson and the many (unfortunately to numerous to name) Voc, CM, HR, Safety, Ergo & Other Pros I know who have also made contributions.

And of course to those staunch supporters in my Writing Club, especially:  Michele C., Doug M., P3, Spike, Kathy McM., Linda A., Kris G., Eric V. KK & KLK, among others.

# Tear out this page and save

## Here are your
## <u>4 Super Secret Simple Steps</u>
## (Cut out page)

Here are the four steps summarized with a bit of advice to really helping yourself in dealing with your workplace injury /pain.

Tear this page out and pin to your wall or carry in your wallet. These four steps will really help you take care of yourself!

1. Understand & take charge of your situation – bull by the horns thing

2. Exercising your rights – "rassle" that concept down and show who's boss

3. Help out your physician and show him how to write a prescription – he'll welcome your help and input, and believe me, you will be helping him do his job in your healthcare

4. The hardest part may be in finding a good, honest Ergo you can believe in, trust and know they will and can take care of you. Alison's article in the Appendix will help you take care of that.

Ergonomic Mis Adventures
Ian Chong CPE
www.ergoinc.com

# Congratulations!!

If you have read made it this far in my book, you probably are a REAL ERGO PRO at some level, credentialed or not.

And you probably have real Ergo in your heart

And for that I thank you, for you have my admiration.

As such, I firmly believe you have it in you to go out and help make this world a better place by taking care of someone's pain, and especially your own (using the 4 secret simple steps).

Godspeed!

---

# Coming Soon!

---

(Surviving)

## *Your Computer as Predator*

*Ways to Address Injury and Pain from
Intensive Computer Usage*

### *Hello: I'm Your Computer and I'm Going to Cripple a Part of You.*

### *I Will Also Provide Answers & Solutions Allowing You to Care for Your Health*

---

*I'm going hurt, maybe even KILL you slowly, painfully and mercilessly. I've done it before and I'll do it again.*

*I will consume small amounts of your flesh, one micro molecule at a time. You will never notice it, or won't even feel it. But succumb you will.*

*Yes, I'm going to hurt you! Minimally, it may just be simple bothersome or maybe even searing, burning pain. At maximum it will ruin your life to be one of bed-ridden debilitating health.*

*(Con't next page)*

*I can destroy your career, your family, your health and maybe even your life.*

*You may think of me as a deadly disease inducing parasite from which there is no escape.*

*My name is BYTR, and YES, I bite. I will do this however I can, whenever I can, simply because you allow me. You see Human, you are the main reason for my existence and for my activity. You have created me and you are the recipient of my lethal actions.*

*I can show you wondrous things. I can perform fantastic feats for you. I am at your beck and call. And yet, within me is the power to destroy important elements of your life.*

*Nevertheless there exist methods and weapons to combat me. However unless you understand them…*

### *YOU ARE TRULY IN PERIL!!!*

*You have been warned…now, you must beware!*

*Be **very** aware, because now…now*

**I AM COMING FOR YOU** -- *it is simply a matter of time. You'll see.*

### *BITE, BITE, BYTE*

### *<u>Watch for answers and solutions to my attacks.</u>*

Made in the USA
Charleston, SC
05 November 2016